COMMUNITY

SALAD RECIPES FROM ARTHUR STREET KITCHEN

BY HETTY MCKINNON

PHOTOGRAPHY BY LUISA BRIMBLE

CONTENTS

7

INTRODUCTION

38

WELCOME TO THE ROOTS

carrots, beetroot, fennel, sweet potatoes

62

EVERYBODY LOVES BRASSICAS

broccoli, cauliflower, turnips, brussels sprouts,
cabbage, kale, cavolo nero, kohlrabi

98

THE KINGDOM OF FUNGI

black fungus, pine, porcini, wild, button

106

THE GOODNESS OF CEREALS

quinoa, pearl barley

112

LOVE, LEGUMES

peas, edamame, lentils

124

HELLO, NIGHTSHADES

tomatoes, eggplant, capsicum

138

MEET THE MARROWS

pumpkin, zucchini, cucumbers

156

IN THE MOOD FOR ASIAN

noodles, seaweed, ginger, tofu, asian greens

ALBION STREET

RILEY STREET

FOVEAUX STREET

CROWN STREET

BOURKE STREET

ARTHUR STREET

DEVONSHIRE STREET

MAP OF
SURRY HILLS

N
W + E
S

INTRODUCTION

There are few things more satisfying in life than cooking a beautiful meal and sharing it with others. To feed people you care about is the ultimate in nurturing and nourishing. At its very heart, food and eating is (or should be) a communal experience that brings together friends, fortifies families, unites neighbours and acquaints strangers.

In our age of ephemera, *Community* invites the reader to find more meaningful ways of connecting through food. This book is not about cooking and eating a meal at lightning pace. Rather, it encourages us all to take the time to find comfort, pleasure, celebration and inspiration in both the process of cooking and the art of eating together.

Why salads? I have come to learn, literally through pedaling a basketful of salads through the streets of my community, that they are the perfect meal to share with others. Pile it up high on a big plate, scatter it on a serving board or, in some cases, pack it in a container, and invite your fellow diners to dig in. The salad is such a versatile dish, can be eaten at room temperature and is totally transportable. Arthur Street Kitchen, with our vegetable-laden recipes, approaches salads as complete meals, not side dishes.

Community is a cookbook to get off the shelf, splatter with food stains and plaster with notes. We hope these recipes will prompt you to try something new or old; a food you like or dislike. Surprise yourself. Embrace the chaos of eating together. Make a mess, splash sauce on the table, dip your fingers in. In messiness, there is satisfaction and happy tummies.

THE STORY OF ARTHUR STREET KITCHEN

People often ask me how Arthur Street Kitchen came about. In all honesty, it is a fairly unorthodox business, with a very humble beginning.

It all started walking the streets of Surry Hills. A few years back, my friend Gabi and I, both vegetable lovers, would meet early every Saturday morning on Crown Street and begin our wander over to a nearby grocer. During that walk, we would talk about our kids, neighbourhood gossip and what we planned for dinner the following week. But our conversations would invariably end up at vegetables and salads. We would rhapsodise over the beauty of eggplant, the sweetness of cauliflower, how bunches of kale would make a beautiful bridal bouquet, and simply marvel at the magic of herbs (don't get us started about herbs!). But in this humdrum dialogue, the concept of Arthur Street Kitchen was born – home-cooked, flavour-packed and hearty salads, the type we ate for dinner most nights, delivered to offices and homes in Surry Hills. This was a simple concept with modest intentions that has somehow given rise to a whole new breed of salad-lovers.

In the autumn of 2011, I started delivering salads to businesses, friends and neighbours in Surry Hills. Soon after, as word spread, I started delivering on wheels – my ubiquitous white bike. As I delivered to more and more people who worked and lived in the community, I discovered that, as much as the business was about local food, it was also about the people who ate the food every week. These are the people who inspire me to cook, and to traverse the laneways and climb the hills week after week with a basketful of salads. Nowadays, I see Arthur Street Kitchen as an extension of my own dining room table. Each week, there is a hunting and gathering of stories and histories, an exchange of ideas. And the best thing about Arthur Street Kitchen is that I get to do what I love most – to feed people!

COMMUNITY

COMMUNITY

COMMUNITY

COMMUNITY

SHINY HAPPY VEGETABLES

'It's not about making statements about vegetarianism. It's just about encouraging people to think creatively about veggies, understand their versatility, feel more confident cooking them well and in turn, eat more of them.'

At the heart of almost every Arthur Street Kitchen recipe is a core vegetable. From this starting point, this vegetable can venture virtually anywhere – teamed with another vegetable, combined with a grain or cereal, transported to another country. This is how an Arthur Street Kitchen salad usually comes to life.

If I had to say I had one aim with this book, it would be to help people rethink vegetables. It's not about making statements about vegetarianism. It's just about encouraging people to think creatively about veggies, understand their versatility, feel more confident cooking them well and in turn, eat more of them. While all the recipes are vegetarian, *Community* is more a 'book of vegetables', showing home cooks how to prepare delicious, hearty, comforting meals without the need for meat.

Community focuses on showing cooks how to utilise vegetables to their full potential. Making the most out of a vegetable can be as simple as, for example, cutting it in a different shape. This may result in more surface area for cooking, which allows for more caramelisation, producing a sweeter taste. Or simply leave the skin on your veg to create more texture. Pumpkins, carrots, potatoes and sweet potatoes are beautiful roasted with their skins on. Simple tricks like these can really change the character of your dish.

Don't be afraid to try new ways of cooking vegetables. Grate them, roast them, pan-fry them, grill them, smoke them, stir-fry them, barbecue them. They all deliver different results that keep vegetables interesting and surprising.

THE LARDER

Tasty salads require thoughtful planning and careful preparation. Having a well-stocked larder is an important part of this process. I have listed in this section the items I think are most useful in a pantry. Don't be scared off by the sizeable list of larder essentials and by no means should you feel compelled to go out and purchase all of them for your pantry right now! You will find that, as you use this cookbook, you will naturally build up an excellent stock of pantry items that will make your everyday cooking so much easier and tastier.

IN YOUR LARDER

GENERAL SUPPLIES

Apple cider vinegar
Balsamic vinegar
Dijon mustard
Dried porcini mushrooms
Extra virgin olive oil
Garlic
Harissa paste
Honey
Pasta
Pomegranate molasses
Powdered vegetable stock
Red wine vinegar
Sea salt flakes (Maldon)
Tahini
White wine vinegar
Whole egg mayonnaise

SPICES I LIKE

Allspice
Bay leaves (dried are fine)
Cayenne pepper
Chilli flakes
Chilli powder
Cinnamon, ground
Cinnamon quills
Cloves, ground
Cloves, whole
Coriander, ground
Coriander seeds
Cumin, ground
Cumin seeds
Curry powder
Fennel seeds
Ginger, ground
Mint, dried
Nigella seeds
Paprika, ground
Paprika, smoked
Paprika, sweet
Peppercorns, black
Peppercorns, white
Sumac, ground
Turmeric, ground
Za'atar

SEEDS & NUTS

Almonds, flaked
Almonds, slivered
Almonds, whole
Hazelnuts
Peanuts, roasted
Pine nuts
Pistachio nuts
Pumpkin seeds
Sesame seeds, black
Sesame seeds, white
Sunflower seeds
Walnuts

ASIAN ESSENTIALS

Ginger
Kecap manis
Mirin
Mung bean vermicelli
Palm sugar
Rice vermicelli
Rice wine vinegar
Sesame oil
Soy sauce
Tamari
Tofu

GRAINS, CEREALS & LEGUMES

Couscous
Farro
Freekeh
Lentils, brown
Lentils, Persian red
Lentils, Puy
Pearl barley
Pearl couscous
Quinoa

CANNED OR FROZEN

Borlotti beans
Butter beans
Cannellini beans
Chickpeas
Edamame beans
Lotus root
Peas

SALAD FUNDAMENTALS

To create a delicious salad, you need to trust your instincts and your palate. Taste, adjust, taste, and adjust again. When in doubt, add a pinch of sea salt and some cracked black pepper. Throw in a soft herb, scatter over a nut. These subtle touches will make all the difference.

I encourage all salad-makers to tap into their own ingenuity. Treat the recipes in this book as a basis for so much more. Swap ingredients around, substitute or replace. Play with flavours from different cuisines. It may seem daunting at first but I have found that some of the best recipes come from the unexpected – I call these the 'accidental dishes' and there are more than a few of these in this book!

At all times, the salads I make at home are seasonal, using whatever fresh produce is available. This makes sense both economically and sustainably, and it ensures that the vegetables you are consuming are at their peak, taste-wise and nutritionally (which gives your salad the best chance of tasting fantastic!). Hence, please be open to substituting vegetables in these recipes whenever you need to. If you can't get pumpkin one week or it's expensive, opt for sweet potato. If turnips are out of season, maybe try a swede or a parsnip. It's all about using the freshest produce at your fingertips.

Most salads are best eaten at room temperature. Eat them straight out of the fridge and you may miss some of the flavours. Some salads, like soba noodles, are fine chilled.

NOTE ABOUT NUTS Adding a humble toasted nut to your salad will give it a striking lift. Toast your nuts in a big batch and keep them in airtight jars in your larder so you can easily add them to finish off your salad or dish. To toast nuts, preheat your oven to a medium setting, about 150°C. Spread them out on a large baking tray and toast for 5–10 minutes. Keep an eye on them to make sure they don't burn. Seeds like white sesame seeds, sunflower seeds and pumpkin seeds can be toasted on the stovetop. Heat a frying pan on medium heat, add your seeds in a single layer and move them around the pan until they take on a golden hue.

HYPE ABOUT HERBS Believe the hype – if I had one piece of advice about salad-making, it would be to make friends with herbs. They will transform your salad from mediocre to magical.

Soft herbs (e.g. parsley, mint, coriander, dill, chives) are essential and there isn't a salad in this book without a herb to finish it. If in doubt about your dish, chucking in a handful of your favourite soft herbs will assuredly bring your salad to life.

--------- **MY FAVOURITE HERB & VEGETABLE COMBINATIONS** ---------

Tomato + basil + oregano   *Beetroot + dill*
Zucchini + dill + mint   *Mushroom + chives + thyme*
Broccoli + parsley + mint   *Pumpkin + sage + coriander*
Brussels sprouts + mint + parsley *Carrot + coriander*
Corn + coriander   *Cauliflower + coriander + dill*

Asian herbs deserve their own special mention. Exotic flavours like Vietnamese mint, Thai basil, perilla leaves, curry leaves, kaffir lime leaves and lemongrass are regulars in my Asian-style salads. They can still be hard to come by in supermarkets or grocers so I encourage you to grow your own Asian herb garden. Most are hardy and super easy to grow, and even the most novice gardener (like myself) can maintain them.

THE ONION ISSUE A spring onion is a shallot is an eschalot! No, they are NOT all the same thing. To further muddy the waters, they are known by different names all around Australia. In this cookbook, for the sake of clarity, the image opposite shows you precisely what I am referring to when I use the terms Chinese shallot, spring onion and eschalot.

Chinese
Shallots

Spring
Onions

Eschalot

COOK'S NOTES

SERVING SIZES The recipes in this book have been written for gatherings so they generally serve about 4–6 people as a main meal. If you are serving as a side dish, the recipes will serve approximately 8–10. If you are cooking for less, please remember to reduce quantities.

MEASUREMENTS The measurements for herbs and salad leaves refer to 'tightly packed' cups.

SEASONING As a general seasoning for cooking water, I use Vegeta Gourmet stock (which is gluten-free). For sea salt, I recommend Maldon brand.

COOKING QUINOA Prior to cooking quinoa, always rinse it well under cold running water – this will take away some of its natural bitterness. I also like to cook my quinoa in salted, slightly flavoured water as this gives the quinoa much more flavour.

EXTRACTING POMEGRANATE SEEDS To remove pomegranate seeds, cut the pomegranate in half, cup it in your hand cut-side down over a bowl and using the back of a knife, firmly tap the pomegranate to loosen the seeds. Remove any of the white membrane.

COOKING WARRIGAL GREENS Warrigal greens contain toxic oxates, which can be harmful if consumed in large quantities. To remove the oxates, blanch in boiling water for approximately 3 minutes and rinse with cold water.

COMMUNITY

COMMUNITY

WELCOME TO THE ROOTS

CARROTS, BEETROOT, FENNEL, SWEET POTATOES

ROASTED BEETROOT WITH CARAMELISED TURNIPS, EDAMAME BEANS AND WASABI MAYONNAISE

Vegetables are my muses. They inspire me to dream, to ponder, to create. But every now and then, a muse emerges in human form, someone who pushes me to try new flavours. This salad was a co-creation with my good friend and salad muse Gabi. She came to me, like an otherworldly light, and whispered 'wasabi mayo' in my ear. The rest was left to me and this is the result. Now an ASK classic.

Preheat the oven to 200°C.

Spread the beetroot over a large baking tray, drizzle with 1 tablespoon of olive oil and season well with salt and pepper. Roast for 40–45 minutes or until tender.

To make the wasabi mayonnaise, place all the ingredients in a bowl and stir to combine. Adjust the amount of wasabi and lime until you get the balance you like.

Heat 1 tablespoon of olive oil in a frying pan on medium heat. Add the garlic, turnips and a pinch of sea salt and fry for 8–10 minutes, turning frequently, until the turnips are juicy and caramelised.

Bring a pot of water to the boil and add some salt. Blanch the edamame beans for 5 minutes or until just tender but still vibrantly green. Drain and refresh under cold running water.

Combine the beetroot, turnips, radishes, edamame beans and shallots and season well with salt and pepper. Toss gently to combine. Serve with spoonfuls of wasabi mayonnaise and sprinkle over the toasted sesame seeds.

SERVES 4-6

8 beetroots (1 kg), peeled and
    cut into 2 cm cubes
3 tbsp extra virgin olive oil
Sea salt and black pepper
1 garlic clove, finely chopped
3 turnips, peeled and cut into
    2 cm cubes
400 g frozen edamame beans
4 radishes, finely sliced
1 cup Chinese shallots (see note
    page 28), finely sliced
2 tbsp sesame seeds, toasted

WASABI MAYONNAISE

1 cup whole-egg mayonnaise
3–4 tsp wasabi paste
Juice of ½ lime
Sea salt

PICKLED BEETROOT WITH PUY LENTILS, BABY SPINACH AND CHEDDAR

Beetroot is such a clever vegetable. I adore its crimson vibrancy and absolute versatility as a salad ingredient. While I love the sweetness of roasted beets and the freshness of grated raw beets, pickled beetroot feels like such a rich, old-world treat. This salad is inspired by one of my favourite salty-and-sweet snacks, pickled beetroot with a slice of strong cheddar cheese.

To pickle the beetroots, scrub and clean the beetroots well. Combine all the ingredients in a large stockpot. Stir and bring to a gentle boil over medium heat. Reduce the heat and simmer for 1–1.5 hours until the beetroots are tender. When cool, peel the beets and cut into 2 cm cubes.

Place the lentils in a saucepan and cover with plenty of cold water. Bring to the boil, turn down the heat and cook for 20–25 minutes or until just tender. Drain.

Heat the oil in a pan and add the eschalots, garlic, sugar and cumin and sauté until tender and starting to brown. While the lentils are still warm, stir through the eschalot mixture, along with a pinch of salt and pepper to taste.

Finely chop the parsley, dill and coriander. Break the cheddar into rough bite-sized chunks.

Spoon the lentils onto a plate and top with the pickled beetroot. Scatter over the spinach leaves, herbs and cheddar. Finish with a drizzle of oil and season well with salt and pepper.

SERVES 4-6

300 g Puy lentils
2–3 tbsp extra virgin olive oil
4 eschalots (see note page 28),
    thinly sliced
1 garlic clove, finely chopped
1 tsp sugar
2 tsp cumin seeds
Sea salt and black pepper
½ cup flat-leaf parsley leaves
½ cup dill fronds
½ cup coriander leaves
200 g aged cheddar
1 cup baby spinach leaves

PICKLED BEETROOT

6 beetroots (750 g)
2 cups white wine vinegar
4 cups water
1 cup caster sugar
1 cinnamon quill
1 star anise
1 fresh bay leaf
3 whole cloves

BEETROOT AND DILL WITH CRÈME FRAÎCHE AND WALNUTS

The combination of beetroot and dill is irresistible. Earthy and refreshing, dill brings beets to life. This salad is inspired by cold borscht soup. Drizzling the beets with balsamic vinegar before roasting intensifies their natural sweetness, while crème fraîche adds a surprising depth of flavour.

Preheat the oven to 200°C.

Place the beetroot on a baking tray and drizzle over the balsamic vinegar and olive oil. Add the garlic, salt and pepper and mix well. Roast for 40–45 minutes or until tender. Remove from the oven and cool.

For the dill crème fraîche, whisk the crème fraîche together with the dill, lemon juice and olive oil. Add a pinch of salt and freshly ground black pepper.

Mix the beetroot with the spring onions and baby spinach leaves and add a good drizzle of olive oil. Season the beets well with salt and pepper. Fold the dill crème fraîche very gently through the beets, to create a vibrant marbled effect. Top with toasted walnuts and sprinkle over more dill.

SERVES 4-6

12 beetroots (1.5 kg), peeled and cut into 2 cm cubes
1 tbsp balsamic vinegar
2–3 tbsp extra virgin olive oil
1 garlic clove, grated
Sea salt and black pepper
3 spring onions (see note page 28), finely sliced
2 cups baby spinach leaves
150 g walnuts, toasted and crumbled
½ cup dill fronds, finely chopped

DILL CRÈME FRAICHE

250 g crème fraîche
½ cup dill fronds, finely chopped
Juice of ½ lemon
1–2 tbsp extra virgin olive oil
Sea salt and black pepper

ROASTED BEETROOT, SHAVED FENNEL AND BROAD BEANS WITH SKORDALIA

Teaming roasted beets with raw shaved fennel and a classic Greek side dish may not seem obvious, but it absolutely works. This dish is all about contrast and texture – sweetness from the beets, freshness from the fennel, earthiness from the broad beans and lemony-garlicky creaminess from the skordalia.

Preheat the oven to 200°C.

Spread the beetroot over a large baking tray, drizzle over 2 tablespoons of olive oil, season with salt and pepper and roast for 40–45 minutes or until tender and sweet. While the beets are still warm, dress them with salt, vinegar and 2 tablespoons of olive oil. Allow to cool.

To make the skordalia, pound the garlic and 1 teaspoon of sea salt using a mortar and pestle. Transfer to a bowl, add the potatoes and bread and stir vigorously to break down the bread. Slowly add the lemon juice and vinegar. Add the oil in a slow, steady stream until incorporated. Season with salt and pepper. Chill until ready to use.

Using a mandolin or food processor, shave the fennel into paper-thin slices.

Bring a large pot of water to the boil, add a pinch of salt and the broad beans. Cook for 1–2 minutes or until just tender. Drain immediately and rinse under cold running water.

Add the broad beans, fennel, parsley and another drizzle of olive oil and toss lightly to combine. Transfer to a serving platter and serve the skordalia on the side.

SERVES 4-6

8 beetroots (1 kg), peeled and
  cut into 1 cm cubes
4–5 tbsp extra virgin olive oil
Sea salt and black pepper
1 tbsp white wine vinegar
3 fennel bulbs, trimmed
400 g broad beans, shelled and
  podded (frozen are fine)
½ cup flat-leaf parsley leaves,
  roughly chopped

SKORDALIA

2 garlic cloves, peeled
Sea salt and black pepper
2 cups mashed potatoes (made
  with 4–5 potatoes)
2 slices stale white bread,
  crusts removed and soaked
  in cold water
2 tsp lemon juice
1 tbsp white wine vinegar
6 tbsp extra virgin olive oil

ZA'ATAR–ROASTED CARROTS WITH KALE, FREEKEH AND BLOOD ORANGE–MAPLE DRESSING

This salad is all about flavour contrasts – fresh and earthy, smooth and crunchy, bitter and sweet. The za'atar gives the carrots a beautiful herbal nuttiness, while the blood orange–maple dressing delivers a gentle hum to the dish. In the absence of blood oranges, Arthur Street Kitchen diner-cum-recipe-tester Maria Gutierrez cleverly suggests substituting the juice of one orange and one ruby red grapefruit.

Preheat the oven to 220°C.

Quarter the carrots lengthways and slice into 6 cm fingers (or whatever shape you like). Place on a baking tray, coat in 1–2 tablespoons of olive oil, season with salt and pepper, and place in the oven to roast. After about 15 minutes, add the sliced red onions to the baking tray and return to the oven. In total, the carrots should take about 25–30 minutes. When starting to crisp and turn golden, remove from the oven and sprinkle over the za'atar and lemon juice.

To make the dressing, whisk together the orange juice, maple syrup, garlic, vinegar, dill and olive oil. Taste and adjust the seasoning until you get a gentle, sweet sauce.

Add the rinsed freekeh to a large pot of well-salted water. Bring to the boil and then simmer on medium heat until the grains are tender. Drain.

In a large frying pan, add 2 tablespoons of olive oil, the garlic and the kale leaves. Season well with a big pinch of salt and pepper and cook until the leaves have wilted.

Combine the carrots and red onion with the kale, freekeh and half the chopped parsley. Pour over the blood orange–maple dressing and gently mix. Sprinkle over the hazelnuts and remaining parsley.

SERVES 4-6

10 carrots (1.2 kg), peeled and sliced
3–4 tbsp extra virgin olive oil
Sea salt and black pepper
1 red onion, finely sliced
1 tbsp za'atar
Juice of ½ lemon
1 cup freekeh grains, rinsed well
1 garlic clove, crushed
1 bunch kale, stems removed and leaves roughly torn
1 cup flat-leaf parsley leaves, roughly chopped
½ cup hazelnuts, roasted, skinned and roughly crushed

BLOOD ORANGE–MAPLE DRESSING

Juice of 2 blood oranges
2 tbsp maple syrup
1 garlic clove, crushed
1 tbsp white wine vinegar
½ cup dill fronds, finely chopped
3 tbsp extra virgin olive oil
Sea salt and black pepper

SPICED ROASTED CARROT WITH FENNEL, CARAMELISED ONION AND HAZELNUTS

No vegetable is more humble than the carrot. Inexpensive and so accessible, carrots lend themselves perfectly to spices. Naturally sweet with a wonderfully robust texture, I love roasting carrots until they take on a charred edge. This recipe gives carrots a kick with a spice paste, along with roasted fennel and sweet, golden onions. Don't forget a squeeze of lime at the end for that extra bit of zest.

Preheat the oven to 200°C.

To make the spice paste, using a mortar and pestle, pound together the cumin seeds and a big pinch of salt and pepper. Add the garlic cloves and thyme leaves and pound until you have a rough paste. Add enough extra virgin olive oil to cover the paste and finish off with red wine vinegar.

Place the carrots on a large baking tray, spoon over the spice paste and coat well. Place in the oven to roast. After the carrots have been roasting for about 25 minutes, add the fennel slices to the same baking tray and stir to coat the fennel in the spice paste. Sprinkle with an extra pinch of salt and return to the oven. Bake for another 20 minutes until the carrots and fennel are golden.

For the caramelised onion, heat the olive oil in a large frying pan and add the sliced onions. Cook for about 10–15 minutes, stirring every now and then, until they are golden and sweet.

Combine the carrots and fennel with the caramelised onions, chickpeas, hazelnuts and chopped coriander. Top with cubed feta, sprinkle over the reserved fennel fronds and serve with lime wedges.

SERVES 4-6

8 carrots (about 1 kg), peeled and sliced diagonally 1 cm-thick
2 fennel bulbs, cut into 5 mm slices (fronds reserved)
Sea salt and black pepper
2 tbsp extra virgin olive oil
2 brown onions, finely sliced
500 g cooked chickpeas (about 2 cans), drained
½ cup hazelnuts, roasted and skinned
3 tbsp finely chopped coriander leaves
100 g feta, cubed
1 lime, quartered

SPICE PASTE

2 tsp cumin seeds
Sea salt and black pepper
2 garlic cloves, peeled
4 thyme sprigs, leaves picked
2–3 tbsp extra virgin olive oil
1 tbsp red wine vinegar

HONEY–ROASTED CARROTS WITH MUNG BEANS AND LABNEH

Honey and carrot is a classic combo, but throw in mung beans and homemade labneh and this dish becomes a modern masterpiece. Learning to make labneh was one of the most useful cooking skills I've ever gained. Make extra to share with friends. It is beyond simple and the results are so impressive. Note that you'll need to start this recipe the day before.

To make the labneh, line a colander or sieve with a piece of muslin or a thin cotton sheet. Mix the yoghurt, garlic and salt and pepper. Spoon the yoghurt into the cloth and secure tightly with an elastic band or tie. Give the bundle a good squeeze over the sink and then put it back into the colander. Sit the colander on a plate and leave it in the fridge for at least 24 hours.

Preheat the oven to 200°C.

Combine the carrots with 3 tablespoons of the honey, 2 tablespoons of the olive oil, the ground coriander, cumin and thyme and season well with salt and pepper. Spread the carrots out on one or two large baking trays and roast for around 40 minutes, stirring a couple of times, until the carrots are tender and glazed. Remove from the oven and, while still hot, drizzle the carrots with an extra tablespoon of honey.

Bring a medium saucepan of water to the boil, add the mung beans and simmer for 20–25 minutes until tender. Drain, shake well and transfer to a large bowl. Heat 3 tablespoons of the oil in a small frying pan and add the chilli flakes and garlic. Cook on medium heat for about 30 seconds and then pour the oil over the cooked mung beans, along with a good pinch of salt and pepper.

Add the carrots to the mung beans, along with the coriander leaves and lemon zest, and toss gently. Transfer to a serving bowl, dot with labneh, drizzle with olive oil and scatter over the pumpkin seeds.

SERVES 4-6

10 carrots (about 1.4 kg), peeled and sliced diagonally 1 cm-thick
4 tbsp honey
5–6 tbsp extra virgin olive oil
1 tbsp ground coriander
1 tsp ground cumin
4 thyme sprigs
Sea salt and black pepper
400 g dried mung beans
½ tsp dried chilli flakes
2 garlic cloves, crushed
1 cup coriander leaves, roughly chopped
Grated zest of 1 lemon
½ cup pumpkin seeds, toasted

LABNEH

500 g Greek yoghurt
1 garlic clove, grated
Sea salt and black pepper

CHARGRILLED FENNEL AND ASPARAGUS WITH PEARL COUSCOUS AND CORIANDER OIL

This is a light yet satisfying salad made extra special by the distinctive, earthy coriander oil. The dash of honey in the oil really softens the pungency of coriander and adds a gentle sweetness to the dish.

To make the coriander oil, blitz together the coriander, olive oil, garlic, chilli and honey in a food processor. Season with sea salt and black pepper.

Place the fennel and asparagus in a large bowl and coat in 2 tablespoons of olive oil, salt and pepper. Heat a barbecue or griddle pan until it is smoking hot. Cook the fennel and asparagus in a single layer until they are tender, with nice char marks. Continue until all the fennel and asparagus slices have been cooked. When the fennel is cool enough to handle, slice into smaller pieces.

Coat the red onion in a little olive oil and add it to the barbecue or pan. Chargrill until the onion is just soft.

Bring a large pot of salted water to the boil. Add the pearl couscous, stir and simmer for 8–10 minutes until the couscous is tender. Drain.

Season the couscous with salt, pepper and lemon juice. Combine the couscous with the asparagus, fennel, red onion and coriander leaves. Drizzle over the coriander oil and mix well. Top with the sunflower seeds.

SERVES 4-6

3 fennel bulbs, trimmed and cut into 5 mm slices (fronds reserved)
2 bunches asparagus, trimmed and cut into 5 cm pieces
2–3 tbsp extra virgin olive oil
Sea salt and black pepper
1 red onion, finely sliced
300 g pearl couscous
Juice of ½ lemon
½ cup coriander leaves
¼ cup sunflower seeds, toasted

CORIANDER OIL

1 cup coriander stems and leaves
150 ml extra virgin olive oil
1 garlic clove, crushed
1 long green chilli, deseeded
1 tsp honey
Sea salt and black pepper

BAKED SWEET POTATO WITH ROCKET, FETA AND BLACK OLIVE–WALNUT RELISH

This is a salad of extreme flavours. Sweet potatoes are teamed with a salty duo of black olives and feta. To up the ante, I like using wrinkly black olives to create an even bigger flavour contrast, but any black olive will work just fine. This relish is also lovely served with barbecued eggplant.

Preheat the oven to 200°C.

Arrange the sweet potato slices on a large baking tray, coat in the olive oil and season well with salt and pepper. Roast for 20–25 minutes or until tender.

In a large saucepan of cold water, add the lentils and bring to the boil over high heat. Reduce the heat to medium and cook for 20–25 minutes until just soft. Drain.

To make the relish, place the walnuts and garlic in a mortar and pound them with the pestle until you have a coarse mixture. Transfer to a bowl and stir in the coriander, olives, oil and a big pinch of salt and pepper. Slowly add in the lemon juice and stir until well mixed.

To serve, combine the sweet potatoes with the cooked lentils, rocket, salt and pepper and toss gently to combine. Crumble the feta and spoon the black olive–walnut relish over the top.

SERVES 4-6

4 sweet potatoes (2 kg), cut into
  1 cm slices
2–3 tbsp extra virgin olive oil
Sea salt and black pepper
300 g Puy lentils
2 cups (80 g) rocket leaves
200 g feta

BLACK OLIVE–WALNUT RELISH

1 cup walnut pieces, toasted
2 garlic cloves, grated
1 cup (30 g) coriander leaves,
  roughly chopped
150 g wrinkly black olives (or
  other black olive), pitted and
  roughly chopped
6 tbsp extra virgin olive oil
Sea salt and black pepper
Juice of ½ lemon

MOROCCAN SWEET POTATO, CHICKPEA AND COUSCOUS WITH CHERMOULA

Chermoula is a punchy North African marinade traditionally used as a seasoning for fresh fish. But I find its complex and fragrant mix of spices a beguiling accompaniment to vegetables, delivering flavour without abandon. Here, the chermoula is beautifully matched with roasted sweet potato and earthy chickpeas, while preserved lemon delivers an undeniable Moroccan touch.

Preheat the oven to 200°C.

Place the sweet potatoes on a baking tray and toss them with 2 tablespoons of the olive oil and a good pinch of salt and pepper. Roast the potatoes, stirring once, for about 20 minutes or until tender.

To make the chermoula, using a mortar and pestle, pound together the garlic, cumin, paprika, cayenne, lemon zest, lemon juice and salt. Transfer to a bowl and whisk in the olive oil until well combined. Stir in the parsley and coriander. Alternatively, you can use a food processor to mix together all the ingredients.

Reduce the oven temperature to 120°C. Place the couscous in a shallow bowl, along with 1 tablespoon of olive oil. Add the vegetable stock to the boiling water and pour over the couscous, stirring well. Cover the bowl with cling wrap and let stand for 10 minutes. Uncover and dot the couscous with butter, cover with foil and heat in the oven for 5 minutes. Remove from the oven and fluff up the grains with a fork.

Combine the roasted sweet potatoes with the couscous, chickpeas, preserved lemon and gently fold through the chermoula. Transfer to a large serving dish and sprinkle over the flaked almonds.

SERVES 4-6

5 sweet potatoes, peeled and cut into 1 cm cubes
3–4 tbsp extra virgin olive oil
Sea salt and black pepper
400 g couscous
2 tsp vegetable stock powder
600 ml boiling water
30 g butter, cubed
500 g cooked chickpeas (about 2 cans), drained
1 tbsp finely chopped preserved lemon
½ cup flaked almonds, lightly toasted

CHERMOULA

2 garlic cloves
2 tsp ground cumin
2 tsp paprika
½ tsp cayenne pepper
Juice and zest of 1 lemon
1 tsp sea salt
3 tbsp extra virgin olive oil
½ cup flat-leaf parsley leaves, finely chopped
½ cup coriander leaves, finely chopped

SPICED SWEET POTATO, PUY LENTILS AND ROCKET WITH HONEY–ROASTED WALNUTS

Sugar and spice and all things nice – this salad is exactly that. The natural sweetness of the potatoes combines perfectly with the warming spices of cumin, cinnamon and nutmeg. And the honey–roasted walnuts are nothing short of show-stopping. Make a double batch and keep them in a jar for snacking!

Preheat the oven to 200°C.

In a large bowl, combine the sweet potato with the olive oil, nutmeg, cinnamon, cumin and allspice and season with salt and pepper. Roast for 25–30 minutes or until tender and starting to turn golden.

Bring a large pot of water to the boil, add the lentils and simmer over medium heat for around 20 minutes or until the lentils are tender but still have a bite to them. Drain.

To make the sweet vinaigrette, whisk together all the ingredients and season with salt and black pepper. While the lentils are still warm, stir through the vinaigrette.

To prepare the walnuts, combine the honey with the chilli flakes, turmeric, salt and just enough water to make a thick paste. Coat the walnuts in the paste and spread onto a baking tray. Roast for 15 minutes until the walnuts are crunchy and almost dry. The nuts will stay a bit sticky which is fine.

Use whatever combination of soft herbs you have available. Parsley, mint, dill, coriander, chervil, tarragon or chives are all fine. Chop the herbs finely.

Combine half the herbs with the rocket, sweet potato and lentils and season well. To serve, scatter over the walnuts, the remaining herbs and the parmesan.

SERVES 4-6

3 sweet potatoes (2 kg), peeled and cut into 2 cm cubes
2–3 tbsp extra virgin olive oil
½ tsp ground nutmeg
1 tsp ground cinnamon
2 tsp ground cumin
½ tsp ground allspice
Sea salt and black pepper
250 g Puy lentils, rinsed
1 cup soft herb leaves (mint, parsley, chervil, tarragon, chives, dill or coriander)
2 cups baby rocket leaves
50 g parmesan, shaved

SWEET VINAIGRETTE

1 tbsp honey
1 garlic clove, grated
2 tbsp red wine vinegar
4 tbsp extra virgin olive oil
Sea salt and black pepper

HONEY–ROASTED WALNUTS

2 tbsp honey
¼ tsp dried chilli flakes
½ tsp turmeric
Pinch of sea salt
2 cups walnuts

EVERYBODY LOVES BRASSICAS

BROCCOLI, CAULIFLOWER, TURNIPS, BRUSSEL SPROUTS,
CABBAGE, KALE, CAVOLO NERO, KOHLRABI

CHARGRILLED BROCCOLI WITH CHICKPEAS, ALMONDS, LEMON AND CHILLI

The first time I tasted chargrilled broccoli, I experienced a vegetable epiphany. It made me realise how delicious vegetables could taste just by cooking them differently. Chargrilling broccoli gives this modest brassica an exciting, moreish edge. For this salad, the smoky broccoli and nourishing chickpeas are given a daring lift with a hit of lemon and chilli, rounded off with the saltiness of capers.

Toss the broccoli in 2–3 tablespoons of the olive oil and season with a generous amount of salt and pepper.

Heat a griddle pan or barbecue until it is smoking hot and add the broccoli. Turn the broccoli florets so they get char marks all over. Continue until all the broccoli is cooked.

Put the rest of the oil in a small saucepan with the capers, garlic and chilli. Place over medium heat for 30 seconds or so until the garlic just begins to turn golden. Take off the heat immediately and pour the hot oil mixture over the chargrilled broccoli.

Combine the broccoli with the chickpeas, spinach leaves, lemon zest, salt and pepper and mix well. To serve, squeeze over the lemon juice and top with the parsley, mint, parmesan and almonds.

SERVES 4-6

2 heads broccoli (1 kg), cut into florets
6 tbsp extra virgin olive oil
Sea salt and black pepper
80 g capers, rinsed and drained
2 garlic cloves, finely chopped
1 long red chilli, thinly sliced
500 g cooked chickpeas (about 2 cans), drained
1 cup baby spinach leaves
Zest and juice of 1 lemon
1 cup flat-leaf parsley leaves, finely chopped
1 cup mint leaves
80 g parmesan, shaved
50 g flaked almonds, toasted

BROCCOLI AND ORECCHIETTE WITH YOGHURT AND PEAS

My favourite thing about this salad is the subtlety of the pea-infused yoghurt sauce. The peas add a lovely mellow freshness to the tart Greek yoghurt, not to mention a charming pastel hue. Use any type of pasta you like, but I love how the ear-shaped orecchiette pasta captures the sauce.

Begin by making the yoghurt dressing. In a food processor, add the yoghurt, garlic, 3 tablespoons of olive oil, half a cup of the defrosted peas and 2 big pinches of salt and black pepper and blitz up until you get a smooth, pale-green sauce. The sauce should be the consistency of pouring cream. If required, add more olive oil.

Cook the pasta in plenty of salted water until al dente. Drain and refresh under cold, running water.

In a large pot of salted boiling water, cook the broccoli for about 3 minutes or until just tender. Just before the broccoli is ready, add the remaining peas to the water and cook for 30 seconds just to warm through. Drain and refresh.

To put the salad together, add the warm pasta to the yoghurt sauce a little at a time, as adding it in one lot may cause the yoghurt to split. Continue adding the pasta to the yoghurt sauce, along with the peas, broccoli and basil leaves. To serve, scatter over the pine nuts and, if using, the dried chilli flakes.

SERVES 4-6

500 g Greek yoghurt
2 garlic cloves, crushed
4–5 tbsp extra virgin olive oil
400 g frozen peas, defrosted
Sea salt and black pepper
500 g orecchiette pasta
2 heads broccoli (1 kg), cut into florets
½ cup basil leaves, roughly torn
1 tbsp pine nuts, toasted
½ tsp dried chilli flakes (optional)

SWEET SESAME BROCCOLI AND EDAMAME WITH QUINOA

The inspiring thing about salads is that you can really play around with flavours, influences, cuisines, textures, or, in some cases, mix them all together. This salad is a bit of a mash-up, but in a fabulous, exciting way! It's a bit Asian with the edamame beans and sesame seeds, it has a Middle Eastern influence with the nigella seeds and big tahini hit and, to top it off, it's also very textural.

To make the sweet sesame sauce, whisk together all the ingredients until well combined. You may need to vary the amount of honey, water and vinegar to get the right consistency and flavour. You are looking for a sweet yet nutty sauce that is easy to pour.

Bring a large pot of water to the boil and add a pinch of salt, the sugar and vegetable oil (this adds to the sweetness of the broccoli). Blanch the broccoli for about 3 minutes or until just tender. Remove and drain, refreshing under cold running water. Add the edamame beans to the same water and blanch until just tender, around 2–3 minutes, then drain and refresh.

In a large pot of salted water, bring the quinoa to the boil. Reduce the heat and simmer for approximately 20 minutes, or until the quinoa is tender and translucent. Drain to remove excess water.

Combine the broccoli and edamame beans with the sesame oil, quinoa, half the seeds and the sweet sesame sauce. Mix through and season to taste. Top with the remaining seeds and coriander leaves.

SERVES 4-6

Sea salt and black pepper
Pinch of sugar
1 tsp vegetable oil
2 heads broccoli (about 1 kg),
  cut into florets
400 g frozen edamame beans
300 g quinoa, rinsed
1 tbsp sesame oil
3 tbsp sesame seeds, toasted
2 tbsp black sesame seeds
1 tbsp nigella seeds
½ cup coriander leaves

SWEET SESAME SAUCE

3 tbsp tahini
Approximately 50 ml water
1 garlic clove, crushed
1 tsp tamari
1 tbsp honey (or less if you
  don't want it as sweet)
1 tbsp apple cider vinegar
2 tbsp mirin
1 tbsp sesame oil
Sea salt

SMASHED CHICKPEAS WITH BROCCOLI AND DUKKAH

The creaminess of the smashed chickpeas, the smokiness of the chargrilled broccoli and the spiced earthiness of the dukkah combine perfectly in this very memorable salad. The dukkah takes a bit of effort to prepare, but it's well worth it – this recipe will make enough for you to keep some extra in a jar or perhaps give to family and friends as a delicious homemade gift.

To make the dukkah, place a small frying pan over medium heat and toast the coriander and fennel seeds for 30 seconds. Add the cumin and peppercorns and heat for another 20 seconds or until they start to pop. Remove and place in a bowl. Reduce the heat to low and lightly toast the sesame seeds and nigella seeds for a minute or so, then add them to the other spices.

Using a large mortar and pestle, pound the hazelnuts until coarsely broken. Add the coriander, fennel, cumin, sunflower, sesame, nigella and black sesame seeds, along with the peppercorns, and pound again. Mix through the salt and paprika. I like the dukkah to remain quite chunky.

For the chickpeas, place the garlic and a big pinch of salt and pepper in the mortar and pound with the pestle until you have a paste. Add the drained chickpeas, a tablespoon at a time, and smash up roughly (if your mortar is too small, use a large bowl for this part). Stir in 2–3 tablespoons of the olive oil, the chilli flakes, lemon juice and yoghurt until you have a nice, chunky consistency.

In a large bowl, coat the broccoli in olive oil and add a good pinch of salt and pepper. Heat a griddle pan or barbecue to high. When smoking hot, lay out the broccoli in a single layer and cook for a minute or so, turning to make sure that it is well charred on all sides.

Spread a thick layer of smashed chickpeas on a serving platter and lay the broccoli on top. When ready to serve, sprinkle over the dukkah and mint leaves, along with a light drizzle of olive oil.

SERVES 4-6

1 garlic clove
Sea salt and black pepper
750 g cooked chickpeas (about 3 cans), drained
3–4 tbsp extra virgin olive oil
½ tsp dried chilli flakes
Juice of ½ lemon
2 tbsp Greek yoghurt
3 heads broccoli (about 1.5 kg), cut into florets
½ cup mint leaves

DUKKAH (MAKES 2 CUPS)

3 tbsp coriander seeds
1 tbsp fennel seeds
2 tbsp cumin seeds
1 tbsp white peppercorns
3 tbsp sesame seeds
1 tsp black sesame seeds
2 tsp nigella seeds
100 g hazelnuts, skinned and toasted
3 tbsp sunflower seeds, toasted
2 tsp sea salt
2 tsp paprika

ROASTED CAULIFLOWER WITH CAPER VINAIGRETTE AND LEMON–PARSLEY PANGRATTATO

There's a serious melody of flavours and textures in this salad. Mellow roasted cauliflower is made brazen with a tangy caper dressing and tempered with herby lemon breadcrumbs. The pangrattato recipe is a great one to have in your repertoire. You can vary the herbs according to your needs and wants, and add it to virtually any vegetable or salad to make it a bit special.

Preheat the oven to 200°C.

To make the pangrattato, add the bread to a food processor and pulse into chunky crumbs. Transfer to a large bowl and add the lemon zest, garlic, oil and a large pinch of sea salt and massage everything together with your hands to make sure the crumbs are evenly coated. Spread on a tray and bake for 10 minutes or until golden. When cool, add the parsley to the breadcrumbs and mix to combine. Store in an airtight container for 1–2 days (when you are ready to eat, you can re-bake the crumbs for 3–4 minutes to make them crispy again).

Toss the cauliflower in the olive oil and some salt and pepper. Roast for 25–30 minutes or until golden.

To make the vinaigrette, mix the capers, garlic, vinegar and a pinch of salt and pepper. Add the olive oil in a steady stream and whisk vigorously to get a thick, creamy dressing. Taste and adjust the seasoning if required.

To serve, combine the cauliflower with the vinaigrette, spinach and tomatoes. Season the salad well with salt and pepper. Top with the walnuts and scatter over the pangrattato.

SERVES 4-6

2 cauliflowers (about 2 kg), cut into florets
2–3 tbsp extra virgin olive oil
Sea salt and black pepper
50 g baby spinach leaves
250 g (1 punnet) cherry tomatoes, halved
½ cup walnuts, toasted

CAPER VINAIGRETTE

100 g capers, roughly chopped
2 garlic cloves, grated
2 tbsp apple cider vinegar
Sea salt and black pepper
6 tbsp extra virgin olive oil

LEMON–PARSLEY PANGRATTATO

250 g stale bread, torn
Grated zest of 1 lemon
2 garlic cloves, grated
2 tbsp extra virgin olive oil
Sea salt
½ cup flat-leaf parsley leaves, finely chopped

SPICED PERSIAN RED LENTILS WITH ROASTED CAULIFLOWER AND YOGHURT

Cauliflower, with its sweet and tender nature, is a modern vegetable icon. This roasted cauli dish is another Arthur Street Kitchen classic. It's one of those full-package dishes, with delicious golden cauliflower, spiced onions and hearty Persian red lentils, brought together with creamy Greek yoghurt.

Preheat the oven to 200°C.

In a large bowl, coat the cauliflower with 3 tablespoons of the olive oil and season with salt and pepper. Spread the cauliflower on a baking tray and roast for 25–30 minutes until golden and starting to crisp up.

Cook the lentils in a large pot of boiling water for about 20 minutes or until just cooked. Drain.

To make the spiced onion, toast the cumin and coriander seeds in a dry frying pan until fragrant. Crush using a mortar and pestle. Heat 1–2 tablespoons of olive oil in a pan and fry the onion until golden. Add the crushed spices and garlic and cook for a further 2 minutes.

While the lentils are still warm, add the spiced onion and a pinch of salt and mix thoroughly. When the lentil mixture is cool, add the cauliflower, yoghurt, spinach, coriander, mint, a drizzle of olive oil and the lemon juice (do not add the yoghurt while the lentils are hot, as it may curdle!). Season with salt and pepper.

SERVES 4-6

2 cauliflowers (about 2 kg), cut into florets
4–5 tbsp extra virgin olive oil
Sea salt and black pepper
250 g Persian red lentils, rinsed
1 tbsp cumin seeds
1 tbsp coriander seeds
2 brown onions, finely diced
2 garlic cloves, finely chopped
400 g low-fat Greek yoghurt
1 cup baby spinach leaves
1 cup coriander leaves, finely chopped
1 cup mint leaves, finely chopped
Juice of 1 lemon

CHARGRILLED CAULIFLOWER
WITH FRIED BUTTER BEANS AND PUMPKIN HUMMUS

Playing around with salad sauces and dressings is so much fun – sometimes you stumble upon the most delightful surprises. Just like here, where I've messed around with hummus, throwing in some naturally sweet butternut pumpkin. The result is a silky, smooth side dish that also makes a lovely dip.

For the pumpkin hummus, place the pumpkin in a saucepan with a splash of water and salt and cover with a lid. Cook over medium heat for 15–20 minutes, shaking the pan every now and then. If the pumpkin dries out, add another splash of water. The pumpkin is ready when it is very soft and falls apart when stirred. Allow to cool.

Combine the pumpkin, tahini, garlic, salt, olive oil, cumin and lemon juice and whisk to break up the pumpkin. Stir in the yoghurt. Adjust the seasoning, adding more salt, pepper, oil or lemon juice as needed.

Heat a barbecue or griddle pan to high. Coat the cauliflower in 2 tablespoons of the olive oil and season with salt and pepper. Cook on the barbecue or pan for 2–3 minutes on each side until charred all over.

Heat the remaining oil in a frying pan on medium heat. Add the garlic, cumin, coriander and a pinch of salt and cook for 10 seconds to release the flavours. Increase the heat to high and add the butter beans to the pan, stirring to coat the beans in the spices. Cook for 5–6 minutes, shaking the pan often, until the butter beans go crispy on both sides.

Combine the roasted cauliflower and butter beans with the herbs. On a large serving dish, place a big dollop of pumpkin hummus and spoon the cauliflower and butterbean mixture on top or to the side. Serve topped with the pumpkin seeds.

SERVES 4-6

2 cauliflowers (about 2 kg), cut into florets
4 tbsp extra virgin olive oil
Sea salt and black pepper
2 garlic cloves, finely chopped
1 tsp ground cumin
1 tsp ground coriander
500 g cooked butter beans (about 2 cans), drained
1 cup flat-leaf parsley leaves, roughly chopped
1 cup coriander leaves
¼ cup pumpkin seeds, toasted

PUMPKIN HUMMUS

750 g butternut pumpkin, peeled and cut into 2 cm cubes
2 tbsp tahini
1 garlic clove, grated
1 tsp sea salt
1–2 tbsp extra virgin olive oil
1 tsp ground cumin
1 tbsp lemon juice
2 tbsp natural yoghurt
Sea salt and black pepper

SMOKY BABA GHANOUSH
WITH ROASTED CAULIFLOWER, LENTILS AND POMEGRANATE

I like my baba ghanoush smoky, charred and blackened. This baba ghanoush recipe is exactly that. Less like a dip and more like mashed-up eggplant, leave it chunky for that lovely creamy texture. The smokiness of the eggplant is a perfect accompaniment to the sweetness of roasted cauliflower and is finished off boldly by the tartness of pomegranate seeds and a few drops of pomegranate molasses.

Preheat the oven to 200°C.

Coat the cauliflower in olive oil and season well with salt and pepper. Place on a baking tray and roast for 25–30 minutes until golden.

To make the baba ghanoush, place the whole eggplants directly on the flame of a gas hob, over a very hot barbecue or under a hot grill until they become very soft and the skin is charred all over. When cool enough to handle, carefully peel the blackened skin off the eggplant. Place the eggplant flesh and any juices into a large bowl and break up with a fork, leaving the pieces quite chunky. Add the tahini, garlic, lemon juice, yoghurt and olive oil and mix with a fork or whisk until combined. Adjust the amount of lemon juice and oil to achieve the right smoky, creamy balance. Season well with a few good pinches of salt and pepper.

Bring a pot of water to the boil and add the lentils. Cook for 20–25 minutes or until just tender. Drain.

Combine the roasted cauliflower, lentils, baby spinach, coriander, a drizzle of olive oil, a good squeeze of lemon juice and season well with sea salt and black pepper. Serve with a big dollop of baba ghanoush, scatter over the pomegranate seeds and drizzle with a few drops of pomegranate molasses.

SERVES 4-6

1 cauliflower (about 1 kg), cut into florets
2–3 tbsp extra virgin olive oil
Sea salt and black pepper
300 g lentils (use brown or Puy, or whichever variety you wish)
1 cup baby spinach leaves
½ cup coriander leaves
Juice of ½ lemon
1 pomegranate, seeds extracted
Pomegranate molasses

SMOKY BABA GHANOUSH

4 large eggplants
4 tbsp tahini paste
2 garlic cloves, finely chopped
Juice of 1 lemon
2 tbsp Greek yoghurt
5 tbsp extra virgin olive oil
Sea salt and black pepper

BALSAMIC BRUSSELS SPROUTS
AND PUY LENTILS WITH PARMESAN AND MINT

To me, the Brussels sprout is the perfect vegetable – delicious, versatile, healthy, refined, aesthetically stunning and full of personality. I adore its earthiness, slight bitterness and strong flavour. The first time Brussels sprouts appeared on Arthur Street Kitchen's menu was a seminal moment. Since that first winter in 2011, Brussels sprouts have remained my number one selling and most loved vegetable.

Preheat the oven to 220°C.

Place the Brussels sprouts on a large baking tray and toss with olive oil and a really good pinch of salt and black pepper. Roast for 25–30 minutes or until golden and crispy. If they start crisping up too much on one side, take them out of the oven and turn them over.

To make the balsamic dressing, whisk together all the ingredients, adjusting the amount of vinegar, oil, salt and pepper until you achieve the right balance.

Bring a pot of water to the boil and add the lentils. Cook for 20–25 minutes or until just tender. Drain.

While the lentils are still warm, combine them with the roasted Brussels sprouts and parsley and drizzle over the balsamic dressing. Season with sea salt and black pepper and mix well. Transfer to a large serving plate and scatter over the mint leaves, shaved parmesan and toasted almonds.

SERVES 4-6

1 kg Brussels sprouts, trimmed
  and cut in half
3–4 tbsp extra virgin olive oil
Sea salt and black pepper
200 g Puy lentils, rinsed
½ cup flat-leaf parsley leaves,
  roughly chopped
1 cup mint leaves
50 g parmesan, shaved
½ cup almonds, toasted and
  roughly chopped

BALSAMIC DRESSING

1 tsp Dijon mustard
2 tbsp balsamic vinegar
6 tbsp extra virgin olive oil
1 garlic clove, grated
Sea salt and black pepper

CHARGRILLED BRUSSELS SPROUTS
WITH LOTUS ROOT AND SWEET MARINATED TOFU

Brussels sprouts, with their slightly bitter character, are very well suited to the richness of Asian flavours. For this salad, I like to chargrill the sprouts on the barbecue to amplify the smoky flavour. Lotus root is available in the frozen section of Asian supermarkets and adds a lovely subtle crunch. If you can't find it, just substitute with another crispy veg like water chestnuts or even snow peas.

To make the marinade, whisk together all the ingredients. Lay the tofu in the marinade and let it sit for 2 hours or even in the fridge overnight. When ready to cook, trim the tofu into smaller triangles.

Depending on their size, cut each Brussels sprout in half or quarters. Place in a large bowl and add 2 tablespoons of the sunflower oil and a good pinch of salt and pepper. Combine well. On a hot barbecue or griddle pan, cook the sprouts for 3 minutes on each side until just tender. Repeat until all the sprouts have been cooked.

In a large frying pan or wok, heat the remaining oil and add the chilli and eschalots and fry for 2 minutes until softened. Next, add the lotus root with a pinch of salt and stir-fry on medium heat for 4 minutes until the lotus root is hot and the eschalots are completely softened. Remove from the pan.

With the same pan still on medium heat, fry the marinated tofu triangles (reserve the marinade for the dressing) for about 2 minutes on each side or until the tofu is nicely caramelised. Allow to cool.

Combine the sprouts, lotus root and tofu. Pour over the remaining marinade, season with a pinch of salt and pepper and toss gently to combine. To serve, scatter with sesame seeds and coriander.

SERVES 4-6

500 g firm tofu, cut into 5 mm slices
600 g Brussels sprouts, bases removed
4 tbsp sunflower oil
Sea salt and black pepper
1 long red chilli, deseeded and finely chopped
4 eschalots (see note page 28), peeled and finely sliced
400 g frozen lotus root, thawed
1 tbsp sesame seeds, toasted
1 cup coriander leaves

MARINADE

1 tbsp sambal oelek
2 tbsp soy sauce
1 tbsp kecap manis
2 tbsp sesame oil
1 tsp rice wine vinegar
1 tbsp maple syrup

TURNIPS, DUTCH CARROTS AND CANNELLINI BEANS
WITH SUNFLOWER-SEED PESTO

When the big bad wolf tried to lure the sage little pigs out of their impenetrable brick house, he tempted them with juicy turnips. Indeed, for all his huffing and puffing, Wolfie was really onto something because sweet, succulent turnips are a temptation I can rarely resist. This salad features pan-fried turnips with equally enticing grilled Dutch carrots, smothered in an earthy sunflower-seed pesto.

To make the sunflower-seed pesto, blitz together the sunflower seeds, basil, parsley, garlic and some salt and pepper in a food processor. Slowly add the olive oil until you have an almost-smooth paste. Vary the amount of oil depending on how runny you like it. I like my pesto quite chunky and strong in flavour. Stir in the parmesan.

Add the carrots to a large bowl and drizzle with 1–2 tbsp of the olive oil (if you are using normal carrots, trim them down into smaller pieces). On a very hot griddle pan or barbecue, add the carrots in a single layer and cook until nicely charred on all sides.

Heat the remaining olive oil in a frying pan on medium heat. Fry the garlic for just a few seconds and then add a single layer of turnips with a good pinch of sea salt and black pepper. Fry for 5 minutes or so, turning often so all sides are lightly golden and the turnips are tender and juicy.

Combine the carrots, turnips, cannellini beans and parsley with the pesto. To serve, sprinkle over the sunflower seeds.

SERVES 4-6

2 bunches (500 g) Dutch carrots (or normal carrots), scrubbed and leaves trimmed
4 tbsp extra virgin olive oil
1 garlic clove, finely chopped
6 turnips, peeled and cut into wedges
Sea salt and black pepper
500 g cannellini beans (about 2 cans), drained
1 cup flat-leaf parsley leaves, roughly chopped
½ cup sunflower seeds, toasted

SUNFLOWER-SEED PESTO

½ cup sunflower seeds, toasted
1 cup basil leaves
1 cup flat-leaf parsley leaves
1 garlic clove, grated
Sea salt and black pepper
120–140ml extra virgin olive oil
40 g parmesan, grated

GINGER–PEANUT KALE WITH TOFU AND QUINOA

This salad comes with a warning: eat at your own risk as it is very addictive. The combination of kale, tofu and ginger-accented peanut sauce is unexpectedly tasty. This salad is for all the peanut butter obsessives who, like me, are often caught surreptitiously sneaking spoonfuls straight from the jar.

For the ginger–peanut sauce, melt all the ingredients in a saucepan over low heat. Stir until you have a smooth, creamy sauce. Add more water if it's too thick. You want the consistency of thickened cream.

Roughly shred the kale and fold it into the hot peanut sauce. The heat from the sauce will wilt and cook the kale.

Season the tofu well with salt and pepper. Heat 1 tablespoon of the oil in a frying pan and fry each slice of tofu until lightly golden on both sides. Allow to cool slightly, then slice the tofu into strips.

Add the remaining oil to the pan and fry the red onion for 10–12 minutes until caramelised and sweet.

In a large pot, add the rinsed quinoa, a pinch of salt, the vegetable stock and enough water to cover the quinoa by 2 cm. Bring to the boil. Turn the heat down to medium–low and simmer until the quinoa is translucent. When cooked, drain the quinoa through a fine sieve or colander.

Combine the peanut kale mixture with the quinoa, tofu and caramelised onion. Transfer to a large serving plate and top with the chopped peanuts.

SERVES 4-6

2 bunches kale (500 g), stalks removed
300 g firm tofu, cut into 5 mm slices
Sea salt and black pepper
2 tbsp extra virgin olive oil
1 red onion, thinly sliced
300 g quinoa, rinsed
2 tsp vegetable stock powder
1 cup peanuts, roasted and roughly chopped

GINGER–PEANUT SAUCE

4 heaped tbsp peanut butter
1 cup water
2 tbsp tahini
2 tsp sesame oil
1 tbsp finely chopped fresh ginger
2 garlic cloves, finely chopped
3 tsp tamari
2 tbsp rice wine vinegar
1 tbsp honey
Sea salt and black pepper

RIBOLLITA SALAD WITH KALE, CAVOLO NERO, FENNEL, TOMATOES, CANNELLINI BEANS AND CIABATTA

The first time I tasted ribollita soup, in an intimate taverna in Siena, Tuscany, was a monumental tastebud moment. Peasant food at its most simple and spectacular, I was entranced by this soup made with stale bread and humble everyday vegetables. This salad pays homage to this classic Tuscan dish, with the best of leafy winter greens. Use whichever greens and veggies are in season.

Preheat the oven to 150°C.

Toss the tomatoes with 2 tablespoons of the olive oil, the balsamic vinegar, thyme sprigs and salt and pepper. Tip onto a baking tray an slow-roast for 1 hour or until the tomatoes are shrunken and sweet.

Roughly chop the cavolo nero and kale. Heat 2 tablespoons of the olive oil in large pan. Add the garlic, cavolo nero, kale and a big pinch of sea salt and sauté until just wilted, but still green.

Heat a griddle pan or barbecue to high. Coat the fennel in 1–2 tablespoons of olive oil and season with salt and pepper. Cook on the hot pan or barbecue until the fennel is tender and has char marks. Once cooked, if the fennel pieces are too large, cut them into thinner strips.

Combine the kale, cavolo nero, beans, tomatoes, fennel, olives and ciabatta. Finish with good drizzle of olive oil, the oregano leaves and shaved parmesan.

SERVES 4-6

8 roma tomatoes, each cut into 6 wedges
5 tbsp extra virgin olive oil
1 tbsp balsamic vinegar
2 thyme sprigs
Sea salt and black pepper
1 bunch cavolo nero, stems removed
1 bunch kale, stems removed
1 garlic clove, finely chopped
2 fennel bulbs, trimmed and cut into 2.5 mm slices
500 g cooked cannellini beans (about 2 cans), drained
100 g black olives (wrinkly or kalamata), halved
200 g fresh ciabatta bread, torn into chunks
¼ cup oregano leaves
60 g parmesan, shaved

CAVOLO NERO AND BORLOTTI BEANS
WITH TOMATOES, CROUTONS AND BASIL CREAM

When the cool change arrives, I start longing for the moody, deep-green leaves of cavolo nero (otherwise known as Tuscan cabbage). In winter, this chic brassica is my go-to leafy green. Cavolo nero is not only great in soups but I also love it roasted or sautéed. This hearty salad is full of rustic charm, bringing together classic Italian ingredients and flavours, rounded off with a smooth basil cream.

Preheat the oven to 180°C.

To make the croutons, toss the bread in 1–2 tablespoons of the olive oil and a few pinches of salt. Roast in the oven for about 10–15 minutes until golden.

To make the basil cream, combine all the ingredients and mix well. Store in the refrigerator until required. This mixture can be made a day ahead.

In a frying pan, add the remaining olive oil, the garlic and sun-dried tomatoes and toss for 30 seconds. Add the cavolo nero and a pinch of sea salt and pepper and pan-fry for about 4–5 minutes until the leaves are wilted and tender.

Combine the cavolo nero mixture, roma tomatoes, croutons and borlotti beans and fold through the basil cream. To serve, sprinkle over the shaved parmesan and basil leaves.

SERVES 4-6

200 g stale sourdough, roughly torn into chunks
2–3 tbsp extra virgin olive oil
Sea salt and black pepper
1 garlic clove, finely chopped
100 g sun-dried tomatoes, finely sliced
2 bunches cavolo nero, stems removed and leaves roughly chopped
12 roma tomatoes, cut into 3 cm slices
500 g cooked borlotti beans (about 2 cans), drained
50 g parmesan, shaved
½ cup basil leaves, torn

BASIL CREAM

160 g sour cream
½ cup basil leaves, finely chopped
50 g parmesan, grated
1 garlic clove, crushed
1 tsp extra virgin olive oil

CABBAGE AND FENNEL WITH PEAS, MINT, PARMESAN AND LEMON

Sometimes in life, and in food, there is sheer brilliance in simplicity. This salad exemplifies this, brightening up an ordinary, everyday vegetable like cabbage with big flavours and plenty of herbage – in this case, mint, parsley, parmesan and lemon. This is a lovely light dish on its own, but it's also rather nice served as a side to a hearty plate of pasta.

For the lemon dressing, whisk the ingredients together in a bowl and season to taste with salt and pepper.

Bring a large pot of water to the boil. Add a pinch of salt and blanch the peas for 1–2 minutes until they are bright green. Drain and refresh under cold running water.

Combine the peas, cabbage, fennel, herbs, chilli and half the parmesan in a large bowl and toss to combine. Add the lemon dressing, season with salt and pepper to taste and toss gently with your hands until the cabbage begins to wilt (this should take 1–2 minutes). Adjust the seasoning and transfer the salad to a large serving dish. Scatter over the remaining parmesan.

SERVES 4-6

Sea salt and black pepper
300 g peas (frozen or fresh)
500 g cabbage, shredded
2 large fennel bulbs, shaved
1 cup mint leaves, torn
1 cup flat-leaf parsley leaves, roughly chopped
1 long red chilli, deseeded and finely chopped
100 g parmesan, finely grated

LEMON DRESSING

4 tbsp lemon juice
6 tbsp extra virgin olive oil
1 garlic clove, finely chopped
Sea salt and black pepper

VIETNAMESE CABBAGE SALAD WITH TOFU, RICE VERMICELLI AND PEANUTS

This unfettered salad is all about clean, simple Asian flavours. It transforms the humble cabbage into something quite exotic and brave. All it takes is a few basic ingredients and a bold attitude to herbs. This tangy dressing is so versatile and can be easily adapted to suit any Asian-style salad.

To make the dressing, whisk together all the ingredients until well combined. Taste and adjust the flavours, adding more salt, vinegar, sugar or oil if necessary.

Soak the rice vermicelli in hot water for about 5 minutes. Drain. Bring a large pot of water to the boil and add a good pinch of salt. Add the vermicelli and cook for just 1–2 minutes until the noodles are soft. Drain immediately and refresh under cold running water.

Heat the oil in a large frying pan. Sprinkle the tofu with a big pinch of salt and pepper and fry in the pan in a single layer. Cook for 2 minutes on each side until golden. Allow to cool, then cut into thin strips.

Combine the shredded cabbage, carrot, tofu, vermicelli, white pepper and herbs in a large bowl. Pour over the dressing and use your hands or a pair of tongs to toss until well combined. Transfer to a serving plate and sprinkle over the peanuts.

SERVES 4-6

300 g rice vermicelli noodles
Sea salt and black pepper
2 tbsp vegetable oil
600 g firm tofu
700 g green or white cabbage, shredded
2 carrots, grated
½ tsp white pepper
½ cup basil leaves
½ cup Vietnamese mint leaves
½ cup coriander leaves
½ cup peanuts, crushed

ASIAN DRESSING

Juice of 1 lime
2 tbsp sesame oil
2 tbsp brown sugar
1 tbsp rice wine vinegar
1 tbsp kecap manis
1 tbsp ginger, grated
1 long red chilli, finely chopped
1 garlic clove, grated
1 tsp sea salt

THAI KOHLRABI AND CABBAGE SLAW WITH APPLE AND CRUSHED PEANUTS

This Asian-inspired slaw is the perfect modern accompaniment to a barbecue. Kohlrabi, with its firm, crunchy flesh, is such a versatile vegetable, taking the humble slaw to a completely new, exciting place. The Asian herbs and the spicy–sweet dressing are real palate pleasers too. You can replace the kohlrabi with another crunchy vegetable such as raw grated beetroot, fennel or carrot, or even try a combination of them. Make it more substantial by adding a few fried tofu strips.

To make the dressing, peel and grate the ginger and whisk together with the remaining ingredients. Taste and adjust the vinegar, oil, sugar and salt accordingly to get a slightly sweet, slightly salty, tangy sauce.

Using a mandolin/box grater/grating attachment on a food processor or simply a sharp knife, cut the kohlrabi into fine julienne strips.

Combine the kohlrabi, cabbage and apple with the dressing and toss well. Season with salt and white pepper, add the herbs and Chinese shallots and toss again. To serve, top with the crushed peanuts.

SERVES 4-6

2 kohlrabi (600 g), peeled
½ cabbage (600 g), finely
 shredded
2 apples (500 g), grated
Sea salt and white pepper
1 cup Vietnamese mint leaves
½ cup Thai basil leaves (or
 regular basil leaves)
½ cup coriander leaves
¾ cup Chinese shallots (see
 note page 28), finely sliced
1 cup roasted peanuts, crushed

ASIAN SLAW DRESSING

3 cm piece of ginger
Juice of 2 limes
2 tbsp sesame oil
1 tbsp brown sugar
1 tbsp rice wine vinegar
1 tbsp kecap manis
1 long red chilli, finely chopped
1 garlic clove, crushed
1 tsp salt

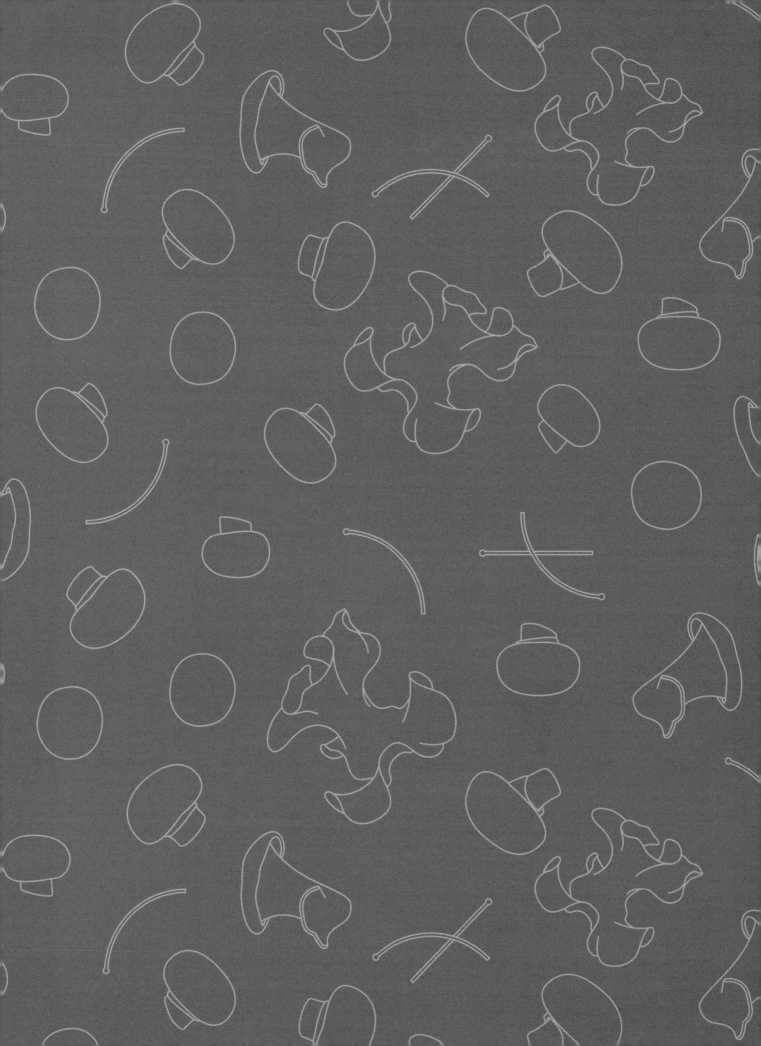

THE KINGDOM OF FUNGI

BLACK FUNGUS, PINE, PORCINI, WILD, BUTTON

BLACK FUNGUS AND FIVE-SPICE TOFU WITH MUNG BEAN VERMICELLI

Black wood ear fungus is a hidden salad gem. Its texture is so distinctive and I love the way it fervently sucks up flavour. And to top it off, the Chinese (my mum especially) swear by its health benefits – from clearing blocked arteries to promoting blood circulation and lowering cholesterol.

To make the dressing, peel and grate the ginger and combine with all the other ingredients in a small bowl. Mix well. Adjust the vinegar, sugar, oil and salt accordingly until you achieve the right balance.

Soak the mung bean vermicelli in boiling water for about 5 minutes. Drain. Bring a pot of water to the boil. Add a pinch of salt and blanch the vermicelli for 1–2 minutes to fully soften. Drain and refresh under cold water.

Soak the black fungus in hot water for about 15 minutes. Drain and dry slightly with a tea towel to remove excess moisture. Carefully pick through the fungus to remove any hard stems or debris and tear larger pieces in half. Heat the vegetable oil in a frying pan or wok, add the fungus with a teaspoon of salt and stir-fry for 3 minutes. You will hear the fungus crackle and pop in the pan, which is normal.

Combine the black fungus, vermicelli, tofu, wombok, Chinese shallots and herbs. Transfer to a large serving bowl, pour over the dressing and toss gently. Top with the sesame seeds.

SERVES 4–6

200 g mung bean vermicelli
Sea salt
90 g black wood ear fungus
2–3 tbsp vegetable oil
220 g (1 packet) five-spice tofu, finely sliced into thin strips
500 g wombok, finely sliced
½ cup Chinese shallots (see note page 28), finely sliced
½ cup coriander leaves, torn
½ cup Thai basil leaves, torn
½ cup mint leaves, torn
½ cup Vietnamese mint leaves, torn
2 tbsp sesame seeds, toasted

ASIAN DRESSING

2 cm piece of ginger
2 tbsp soy sauce
1 tbsp sesame oil
1 tbsp extra virgin olive oil
1 tbsp black vinegar
½ long red chilli, finely chopped
1 garlic clove, grated
1 tsp caster sugar
1 tsp sea salt

PINE MUSHROOMS WITH ESCHALOTS, CHERRY TOMATOES AND SOURDOUGH CROUTONS

If there was a monarch of my vegetable world, it would definitely be the pine mushroom. But blink and you'll miss them, as they are only in season for a short time during autumn and early winter. I am completely enchanted by their earthy, robust flavour, saffron-hued prettiness and, for want of a better description, 'meaty' texture. For this dish, I've teamed this ethereal fungus with eschalots and hearty sourdough croutons in a simple yet stunning autumnal salad.

Preheat the oven to 180°C.

SERVES 4-6

Lay the bread on a large baking tray, coat in 2 tablespoons of the olive oil, sprinkle with sea salt and black pepper and toss well with your hands. Bake in the oven for 15 minutes or until the croutons are golden and crunchy.

Cut the mushrooms into thick slices. Melt half the butter and the remaining olive oil in a large frying pan. Add the garlic and eschalots and cook for 3–4 minutes on medium heat or until soft. Next, add the mushrooms and thyme and season well with a big pinch of salt and black pepper. Sauté for 5 minutes until the mushrooms are starting to soften, then add the cherry tomatoes and cook for a further 5 minutes until the mushrooms are golden and the tomatoes are soft. Repeat until all the mushrooms have been cooked. Turn off the heat and add the remaining butter with a generous squeeze of lemon juice. Check the seasoning, adding more salt and pepper if needed. When cool, add the chopped parsley.

Combine the mushroom and tomato mixture with the croutons and baby spinach. To serve, scatter with parmesan.

500 g stale sourdough, cut into 1 cm slices and torn into smaller chunks

4 tbsp extra virgin olive oil

Sea salt and black pepper

1 kg pine mushrooms, trimmed and wiped clean with a damp cloth

50 g butter, cubed

2 garlic cloves, crushed

6 eschalots (250 g) (see note page 28), thinly sliced

4 thyme sprigs

250 g cherry tomatoes, halved

Juice of ½ lemon

½ cup flat-leaf parsley leaves, roughly chopped

2 cups baby spinach (120 g)

100 g parmesan, shaved

MIXED MUSHROOMS WITH FARRO, FETA AND ALMONDS

For a vegetarian, getting creative with mushrooms is a vital skill. Be bold with your flavours as mushrooms are super soakers and love to be seasoned. For this salad, use whatever mixed mushies you can get your hands on. A few different varieties such as oyster, shiitake, pine or enoki will add extra interest and texture, but even plain old button mushrooms will do the job.

Slice or break up the mushrooms, depending on their size. Smaller mushrooms can be left whole. Heat a large frying pan over medium heat. Add half the butter, the olive oil and garlic. When the butter has melted, add the mushrooms to the pan, along with the whole thyme sprigs, and season well with two big pinches of sea salt and black pepper. Turn up the heat to high and fry for 8–10 minutes, turning the mushrooms around in the pan often. Continue to cook until all the juices have evaporated and the mushrooms are golden. Turn off the heat and add the remaining butter, juice of half a lemon and season to taste with salt and pepper.

Place the farro in a large saucepan with plenty of water. Bring to the boil, add a big pinch of salt and cook for 25–30 minutes until the grains are al dente. Drain.

Combine the farro with the mushrooms and herbs. Taste and adjust by adding more lemon juice, a couple glugs of olive oil, salt and pepper. Transfer to a large serving plate and top with the crumbled feta and slivered almonds.

SERVES 4-6

1 kg mixed mushrooms (for example, oyster, shimeji, fresh shiitake, pine, enoki)

20 g dried porcini mushrooms, soaked in hot water

50 g butter, cubed

2–3 tbsp extra virgin olive oil

2 garlic cloves, crushed

4 thyme sprigs

Sea salt and black pepper

Juice of 1 lemon

400 g farro, rinsed

1 cup flat-leaf parsley leaves, finely chopped

½ cup dill fronds, finely chopped

½ cup tarragon leaves, finely chopped

200 g feta, crumbled

½ cup slivered almonds, toasted

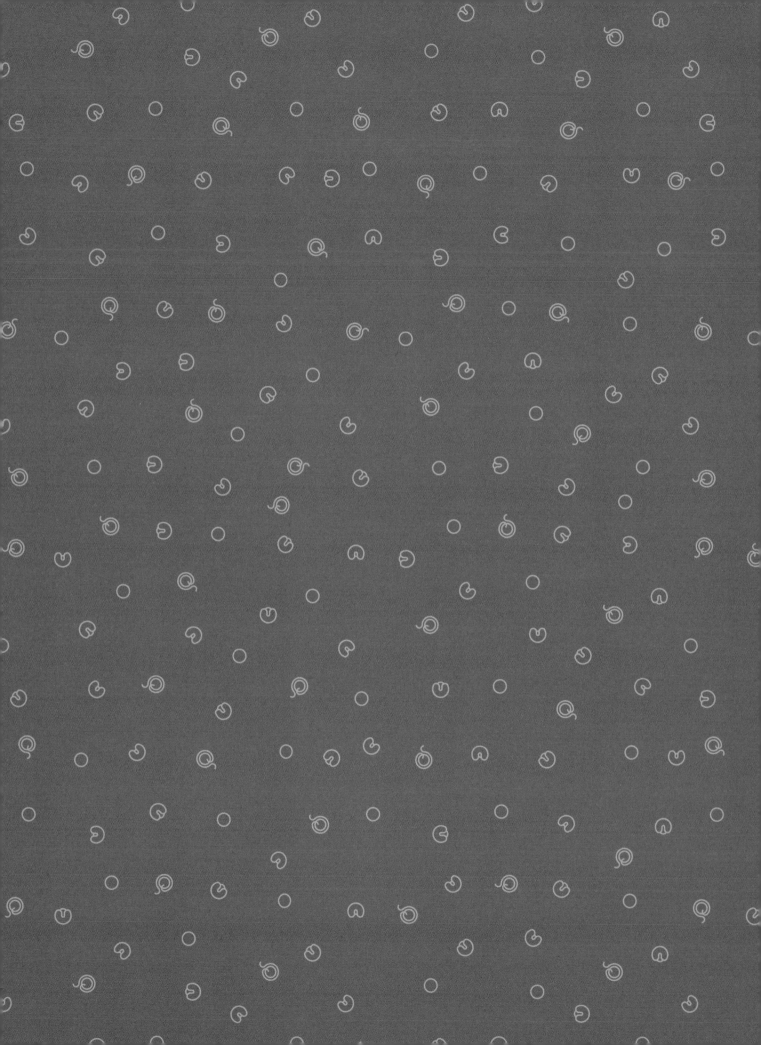

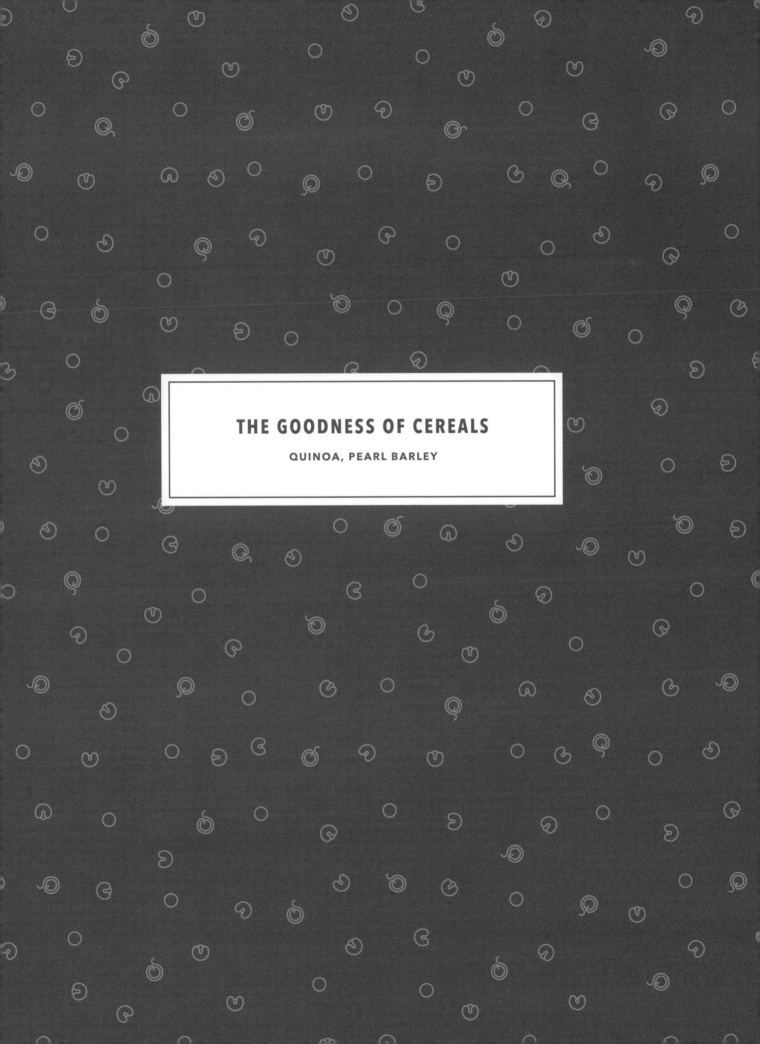

THE GOODNESS OF CEREALS

QUINOA, PEARL BARLEY

WINTER TABBOULEH WITH QUINOA, SUMAC CAULIFLOWER, POMEGRANATE AND FETA

For a purist, tabbouleh is predominantly a parsley salad, accentuated with mint, spring onions, ripe tomatoes and a small scattering of cracked wheat. This recipe is certainly not a traditional take on this Middle Eastern classic, but it is a heartier version for the cooler months, teamed with golden roasted cauliflower. If you're short on time, use a food processor to chop your herbs, but I love the cathartic process of chopping by hand – the result is a lighter, less soggy salad.

Preheat the oven to 200°C.

Coat the cauliflower in 2 tablespoons of the olive oil, salt and pepper. Roast for 25–30 minutes or until the florets are golden. When ready, take out of the oven and, while still hot, sprinkle with the sumac.

Fill a large pot with water and add a pinch of salt and the vegetable stock. Add the quinoa and bring to the boil. Turn the heat down to medium and simmer until the quinoa is tender and translucent. Drain through a fine sieve to remove excess water.

Finely dice the tomatoes and add to a large bowl, along with any juices. Bunch the parsley together tightly and, with a sharp knife, chop the leaves and stems as finely as possible. Finely chop the mint leaves and Chinese shallots. Add the parsley, mint and shallots to the tomatoes.

Combine the quinoa, allspice, lemon juice, tomatoes and herbs with the remaining olive oil, salt and pepper. Add more lemon juice, oil or salt and pepper to get the right balance.

To serve, pile the tabbouleh on a platter. Top with the roasted sumac cauliflower and sprinkle over the pomegranate seeds and crumbled feta.

SERVES 4-6

1 large cauliflower (about 1 kg), cut into florets
6–7 tbsp extra virgin olive oil
Salt and black pepper
2 tsp sumac
2 tsp vegetable stock powder
250 g quinoa, rinsed
6 roma tomatoes (500 g)
4 large bunches flat-leaf parsley
2 bunches mint, leaves picked
4 Chinese shallots (see note page 28)
1 tsp ground allspice
Juice of 1 lemon
1 pomegranate, seeds extracted
100 g feta, crumbled

PEARL BARLEY WITH PISTACHIOS, ROCKET AND BASIL OIL

Most people associate pearl barley with thick winter soups but this humble grain has so much more to offer. It's full of fibre and protein, and is very moreish when used in salads. Pearl barley is also very good at soaking up flavours, so it's wonderful teamed with scented oils. In this salad I've used basil oil, but you can mix things up by using different herbs such as parsley, coriander or mint.

To make the basil oil, place the garlic, salt and pepper in a mortar and pound with the pestle until you have a paste. Add the basil leaves and continue to pound until you have a thick green paste. With your pestle, slowly stir through the olive oil. Alternatively, blitz all the ingredients in a blender or small food processor. This oil can be stored in a clean jar for up to a week.

Place the pearl barley in a large saucepan with plenty of salted water. Bring to the boil and cook for 30–35 minutes. It should remain slightly chewy in texture. Drain.

While the pearl barley is still warm, add the basil oil and mix well. Season well with salt and pepper.

To serve, combine the barley with the rocket and basil leaves. Drizzle over the olive oil. Finish with the marinated feta and a scattering of pistachios over the top.

SERVES 4-6

400 g pearl barley
Sea salt and black pepper
2 cups baby rocket leaves
¼ cup basil leaves
1–2 tbsp extra virgin olive oil
150 g marinated feta
1 cup pistachios, toasted and
  roughly chopped

BASIL OIL

1 garlic clove
Sea salt and black pepper
1 cup basil leaves
½ cup extra virgin olive oil

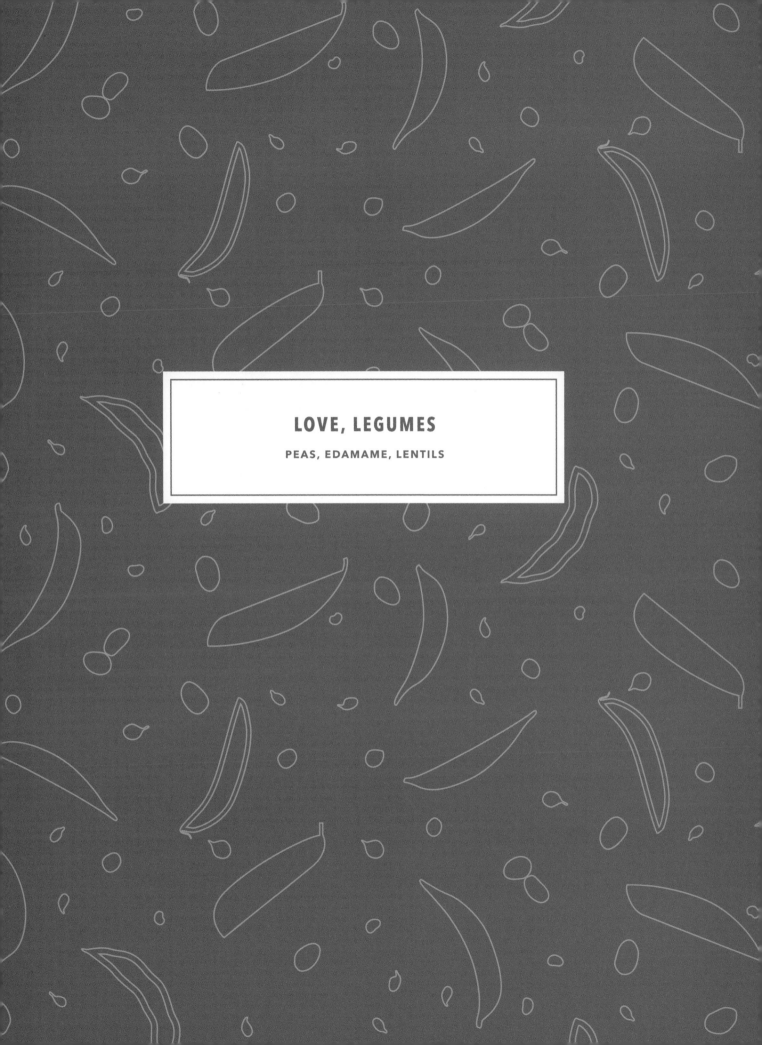

LOVE, LEGUMES

PEAS, EDAMAME, LENTILS

SPICY FRIED EDAMAME WITH EGGPLANT AND SOBA NOODLES

This sticky-cum-spicy sauce takes edamame beans to new flavour heights. Buy edamame podded and frozen from the Asian supermarket and simply steam or boil them for a fortifying and satisfying snack. I use a vegetarian stir-fry sauce in this recipe but if you don't mind ocean creatures, feel free to substitute with regular oyster sauce. The roasted eggplant adds a pleasing silkiness to this salad.

Preheat the oven to 200°C.

Partially peel the eggplant, leaving a 'stripe' pattern. Cut into 2 cm cubes. Drizzle over the olive oil and season with salt and pepper. Roast for 20–25 minutes or until tender.

In large pot of boiling salted water, cook the soba noodles for 3 minutes, stirring constantly to prevent sticking. Drain and refresh under cold running water.

Heat the sunflower oil in a frying pan over high heat. Add the garlic, chilli and ginger and stir-fry for about 1 minute. Next, add the edamame beans and stir-fry for 1 minute. Finally, add the soy sauce, stir-fry sauce and sesame oil and cook for another minute or so, or until the sauce thickens slightly.

Combine the spicy edamame with the roasted eggplant and soba noodles. Toss gently to combine. Serve with a sprinkle of black sesame seeds.

SERVES 4-6

4 eggplants (1.5 kg)
2 tbsp extra virgin olive oil
Sea salt and black pepper
400 g soba noodles
3 tbsp sunflower oil
2 garlic cloves, finely chopped
1–2 long red chillies (depending on how hot you like it), finely chopped
4 cm piece of ginger, peeled and grated
400 g frozen podded edamame beans, thawed
4 tbsp soy sauce
2 tbsp vegetarian stir-fry sauce (or oyster sauce)
1 tbsp sesame oil
1 tbsp black sesame seeds

BALSAMIC–ROASTED PEARS WITH LENTILS, GORGONZOLA AND SAGE

This salad celebrates the magical union that is pears and blue cheese. Use whatever pears are in season, though I do like Packhams as they have a rich flavour and hold their shape well when cooked.

Preheat the oven to 200°C.

Place the pear slices, 2 tablespoons of the oil, white balsamic and sugar on a baking tray and toss gently to coat. Roast for 15–20 minutes or until the pear slices start to turn golden. Set aside to cool.

Place the lentils in large pot of water. Bring to the boil, reduce the heat to medium and simmer for 20 minutes or until lentils are just tender. Drain.

In a frying pan, melt the butter on medium heat until it froths. Throw in the dry sage leaves with a pinch of salt and fry until the leaves become crispy and the butter turns brown.

Combine the pears, lentils and rocket, season with salt and pepper, drizzle over the remaining olive oil and toss gently to combine. To serve, crumble over the gorgonzola and spoon over the crispy sage leaves and any leftover brown butter.

SERVES 4-6

6 Packham pears (1 kg), cored and sliced into 8 pieces
4–5 tbsp extra virgin olive oil
2 tbsp white balsamic vinegar
2 tsp caster sugar
250 g lentils (whichever variety you like)
30 g butter, cubed
1 cup sage leaves
Sea salt and black pepper
2 cups rocket leaves
200 g gorgonzola

PUY LENTILS WITH BALSAMIC–SOAKED FIGS, WATERCRESS AND WALNUTS

Caramelised balsamic is expensive to buy but ever so cheap and easy to make at home. You can prepare a big batch and store it in the pantry – it's wonderful drizzled over a bed of simple salad leaves, roasted tomatoes, grilled vegetables or even roasted meats.

To make the caramelised balsamic, place the vinegar and sugars into a small saucepan and heat on low until the sugars have dissolved. Turn the heat up to high until boiling and cook for 5–10 minutes until the mixture has thickened slightly (it should reduce by about half). Test it by placing a small amount on a cold spoon – it should look darker and run off the spoon less easily. This is also a good opportunity to test it for sweetness, adding more sugar if you desire. It will thicken further upon cooling.

Place the fig slices in a small bowl and pour over just enough caramelised balsamic to cover them. Leave to soak for at least 1 hour, even longer if time permits. Soaking overnight will produce the most lusciously sweet, plump figs.

To make the dressing, whisk together all the ingredients.

In a large pot of water, bring the lentils to the boil. Reduce the heat to medium and cook for 20–25 minutes until the lentils are just tender. Drain.

While the lentils are still warm, add the balsamic dressing and stir through. Add the figs and all the soaking syrup, the herbs and the watercress to the lentils and toss gently. Season to taste. Transfer to a serving dish and scatter over the feta and walnuts.

SERVES 4-6

12 Turkish dried figs, sliced
300 g Puy lentils, rinsed
½ cup dill fronds, finely chopped
½ cup coriander leaves, finely chopped
½ cup mint leaves, finely chopped
½ cup flat-leaf parsley leaves, finely chopped
2 cups watercress (or rocket leaves)
Sea salt and black pepper
100 g feta, diced
1 cup walnuts, toasted and crushed

CARAMELISED BALSAMIC

250 ml balsamic vinegar
4 tbsp brown sugar
6 tbsp caster sugar

BALSAMIC DRESSING

1 garlic clove, crushed
2 tbsp balsamic vinegar
4 tbsp extra virgin olive oil
Sea salt and black pepper

PEAS AND MINT WITH QUINOA, FETA AND ALMONDS

Pea and mint are a love-at-first-sight food match – they belong together, happily ever after. This salad is another Arthur Street Kitchen favourite. The sweet and crisp medley of sugar snaps, snow peas and garden peas is given a kick by a daring double-dose of mint, both in the dressing and as leaves in the salad. As always, use frozen peas if you prefer.

To make the dressing, blitz all the ingredients in a food processor and season with salt and black pepper. Taste for balance, adjusting the vinegar, oil and seasoning as required. For a stronger mint flavour, add a few more leaves.

Bring a large pot of water to the boil and add a large pinch of salt, the sugar and oil (these keep the peas green and enhance sweetness). Add the peas, sugar snap peas and snow peas and blanch for 1–2 minutes or until just tender. Remove and refresh under cold water.

In a large pot of water, add the vegetable stock powder, a pinch of salt and the quinoa and bring to the boil. Turn the heat down to low and continue to simmer until the quinoa is tender and transparent. Drain through a fine sieve.

To serve, add the dressing to the mixed peas, mint and quinoa and combine well. Top with the crumbled feta and almonds.

SERVES 4-6

Sea salt
1 tsp sugar
1 tsp cooking oil
200 g garden peas, freshly
    podded (or frozen)
300 g sugar snap peas, trimmed
300 g snow peas, trimmed and
    sliced in half diagonally
1 tsp vegetable stock powder
400 g quinoa, rinsed
¾ cup mint leaves, torn
100 g Greek feta, crumbled
50 g almonds, toasted and
    roughly chopped

MINTY DRESSING

2 tbsp white wine vinegar
160 ml olive oil
4 tbsp vegetable oil
1 garlic clove, finely chopped
½ tsp caster sugar
½ cup mint leaves
Sea salt and black pepper

SUGAR SNAP PEAS, JERUSALEM ARTICHOKES, CANNELLINI BEANS AND ORECCHIETTE WITH WARRIGAL GREEN PESTO

Warrigal greens, which are a native Australian bush tucker food, actually grow beautifully in urban surroundings. I have a bountiful supply right outside my house in our inner city verge garden. One of my favourite ways to use warrigal greens is in pesto sauces as they add a subtle earthy quality. If you can't get your hands on warrigal greens, simply substitute with English spinach leaves.

Preheat the oven to 200°C.

Working quickly to stop the artichokes turning brown, cut them in halves or quarters lengthways, about 1 cm-thick. Combine with the thyme, a pinch of salt and pepper and 2 tablespoons of the olive oil and coat well. Roast for about 35 minutes, or until tender and lightly golden. If required, turn after 15 minutes.

For the pesto, bring a small pot of water to the boil and add the warrigal greens. Blanch for 3 minutes, then rinse immediately in cold running water. Blitz the garlic, warrigal greens, basil and pumpkin seeds in the food processor. Slowly drizzle in the olive oil until you have a smooth sauce. Stir in the parmesan and add salt and pepper to taste.

Bring a large pot of salted water to the boil and add the sugar snap peas. Cook for only 1 minute, as you want them to stay vibrantly green and crunchy. Remove immediately and rinse under cold water.

In the same pot of boiling water, add the pasta and stir. Cook for about 12 minutes or until the orecchiette is al dente. Drain and refresh.

Combine the sugar snap peas, artichokes, cannellini beans and orecchiette and stir through the warrigal green pesto. Transfer to a serving plate and top with the pumpkin seeds and basil leaves.

SERVES 4-6

600 g Jerusalem artichokes, scrubbed well
4 thyme sprigs
Sea salt and black pepper
3 tbsp extra virgin olive oil
300 g sugar snap peas, trimmed
500 g orecchiette pasta
400 g cooked cannellini beans (about 2 cans), drained
½ cup pumpkin seeds, toasted
½ cup basil leaves, torn

WARRIGAL GREEN PESTO

2 cups warrigal greens, picked (see Cook's Notes on page 33)
1 garlic clove, sliced
1 cup basil leaves
½ cup pumpkin seeds, toasted
200 ml extra virgin olive oil
70 g parmesan, grated
Sea salt and black pepper

HELLO, NIGHTSHADES

TOMATOES, EGGPLANT, CAPSICUM

BAKED TOMATOES WITH CAPERS, OLIVES AND CROUTONS

As a tomato devotee, I am always looking for tasty ways of eating them all year round. This is one of my all-time favourite tomato salads, particularly during the cooler months. Tomatoes baked in seasoned crème fraîche and teamed with crunchy croutons. This is a finger-lickin', mop-it-up salad.

Preheat the oven to 180°C.

Cut the tomatoes into 3 cm pieces, in whatever shape you like. Place in a large bowl and add the crème fraîche, sugar, half the capers, rosemary, garlic, 1–2 tablespoons of the oil and half the grated parmesan. Toss together to coat the tomatoes and season well. Place on a tray and bake for 20 minutes until the tomatoes start to crisp up. Remove from the oven and allow to cool slightly.

Cut the bread into 3 cm squares and coat in the remaining oil and a pinch of salt. Place on a large tray and bake for around 15 minutes, or until the bread is lightly golden. Remove from the oven and allow to cool slightly.

Combine the tomatoes with the olives and croutons. If you have the time, let the salad sit for about 30 minutes to allow the flavours to intensify and the croutons to soak up the rich tomato juices. To serve, scatter over the basil and oregano leaves and the remaining grated parmesan and capers.

SERVES 4-6

10 firm, ripe tomatoes (1.5 kg) (any variety)
250 g crème fraîche
1 tbsp brown sugar
60 g capers, roughly chopped
2 rosemary sprigs, leaves picked and finely chopped
2 garlic cloves, grated
3–4 tbsp extra virgin olive oil
100 g parmesan, finely grated
Sea salt and black pepper
500 g stale sourdough (or other bread), cut into 1 cm slices
100 g olives (any variety), pitted and halved
½ cup basil leaves, torn
2 tbsp oregano leaves

PANZANELLA WITH HEIRLOOM TOMATOES

This Florentine dish celebrates the abundance of summer in the most provident of ways – stale bread, soaked in the juice of ripe tomatoes and accented simply with good quality extra virgin olive oil and vinegar. Just make sure you use the best and fairest tomatoes you can get your hands on and choose your favourite type of bread – be it sourdough, ciabatta, or another crusty loaf.

Preheat the oven to 180°C.

Place the bread on a large baking tray and drizzle over 2 tablespoons of the oil and a pinch of sea salt. Bake for 15 minutes or until the bread is golden and crispy.

Depending on the size of the tomatoes, halve or quarter them so you have a mix of shapes and sizes. Combine the tomatoes and red onion in a bowl and season well with salt and pepper.

Combine the bread and tomato mixture in a large mixing bowl. Using your hands, toss well, gently squeezing the tomatoes – this will extract more juice for the bread to soak up. Drizzle over the remaining oil and the vinegar, add the basil and parsley and toss thoroughly. Let the salad sit for about 30 minutes before serving. (This allows the flavours to develop. If you don't have time, eat straight away!) To serve, scatter over the shaved parmesan.

SERVES 4-6

400 g stale bread, cut or torn into chunks
4 tbsp extra virgin olive oil
Sea salt and black pepper
500 g heirloom tomatoes (or other ripe tomato)
1 red onion, very finely sliced
1 tbsp balsamic vinegar
1 cup basil leaves
½ cup flat-leaf parsley leaves
½ cup parmesan, shaved

SLOW-ROASTED BALSAMIC TOMATOES
WITH SPELT PASTA, PORCINI AND RICOTTA

One of the most satisfying kitchen moments is the 'accidental dish' – the unplanned meal thrown together with scarce larder ingredients that somehow turns into a resounding culinary success. This is one of those dishes. With the help of a few herby accents from the garden, the intensely sweet slow-roasted tomatoes and the ricotta combine to form a fruity, creamy sauce. The little drizzle of caramelised balsamic at the time of serving really brings the whole dish together.

Preheat the oven to 140°C.

In a large mixing bowl, combine the tomatoes, balsamic vinegar, 2 tablespoons of the olive oil, thyme, 1 clove of grated garlic and season well with salt and pepper. Roast in the oven for 1–1.5 hours until the tomatoes are shrunken and juicy.

In a large pot of salted boiling water, cook the spelt pasta (or whatever pasta you are using) according to packet instructions.

In a small frying pan, melt the butter, add the remaining grated garlic and cook for 10 seconds until fragrant. Remove the mushrooms from the water and add to the pan, along with a couple teaspoons of their soaking liquid (making sure not to include any of the grit) and a good pinch of sea salt and black pepper. Cook for 2 minutes until the water has evaporated.

Combine the tomatoes, pasta and mushrooms and season well with salt and black pepper. Break the ricotta into chunks and gently fold through the pasta. To serve, scatter over the basil and oregano leaves and finish with a drizzle of caramelised balsamic vinegar and the remaining olive oil.

SERVES 4-6

10 roma tomatoes (1.4 kg),
   each cut into 8 wedges
2 tbsp balsamic vinegar
4 tbsp extra virgin olive oil
4 thyme sprigs
2 garlic cloves, grated
Sea salt and black pepper
500 g spelt pasta (or your
   favourite pasta shape)
10 g butter
30 g dried porcini mushrooms
   (or other dried mushrooms),
   soaked in hot water
250 g ricotta
½ cup basil leaves, torn
¼ cup oregano leaves
2 tbsp caramelised balsamic
   vinegar (see page 119 for
   recipe)

BLACK BEAN EGGPLANT WITH SNAKE BEANS AND BROWN RICE

Food from my childhood inspires many of my salads. This salad is a nod to my mum's delicious Cantonese cooking and features one of my favourite condiments – black bean sauce. This sauce can be kept in the fridge for up to two weeks. You can also use normal eggplant if the Japanese variety is not available and substitute green beans when snake beans are out of season.

To make the sauce, first drain the black beans. Heat a wok or large frying pan over high heat. Add 125 ml of the oil and swirl to coat the pan. Add the black beans, garlic, ginger and shallots and stir-fry for 2 minutes or until the mixture has softened. Reduce the heat to medium, add the sambal oelek and wine and cook until the sauce has thickened slightly. Remove from the heat and check the seasoning, adding a little sea salt and black pepper if needed. Transfer half the sauce to a blender and puree while adding the remaining oil. Stir the puree back into the remaining mixture and allow to cool.

Next, cook the eggplant in batches. Heat a wok or frying pan on high. Add some oil and eggplant to the pan and stir to coat well. Place a lid on the wok, turn the heat down to medium and cook for 5–6 minutes, stirring once or twice. Continue until all the eggplant has been cooked. Next, stir in the beans and 2 cups of the black bean sauce. Replace the lid and allow to cook for another 7–8 minutes or until the eggplant and beans are tender. Lastly, add the brown rice and toss well.

To serve, place the eggplant and rice on a large plate, season well and scatter over the shallots.

SERVES 4-6

125 ml vegetable oil
12 Japanese eggplants (or 4 regular eggplants), cut into 2 cm pieces
150 g snake beans (or green beans), trimmed and cut into 5 cm pieces
4 cups cooked brown rice, cold
Sea salt and black pepper
½ cup Chinese shallots (see note page 28), finely chopped

BLACK BEAN SAUCE (MAKES 1 L)

1 cup (130 g) salted black beans, washed and soaked for 5 mins to soften
375 ml rice bran oil (or other neutral oil)
2 garlic cloves, finely chopped
2 tbsp grated ginger
2 cups Chinese shallots (see note page 28), trimmed and finely sliced
1 tbsp sambal oelek (or hot chilli sauce)
4 tbsp Shaoxing rice wine
Sea salt and black pepper

MISO EGGPLANT WITH SOBA NOODLES AND WALNUTS

Miso is the perfect balance of salty, sweet, fruity and savoury. This sheer complexity of flavour is like no other and is a formidable match for the full-bodied silkiness of eggplant. Roasting the eggplants makes this a much healthier alternative to traditional Japanese deep-fried miso eggplant. But beware, this dish is super addictive – it's a hands-down Arthur Street Kitchen cult classic.

Preheat the oven to 200°C.

Peel strips of skin from the eggplant, from top to bottom, so it leaves a stripy pattern. Cut into 2 cm cubes and place on a baking tray. Drizzle with 3 tablespoons of the olive oil and roast for 20–25 minutes or until tender. Remove from the oven, place in a colander, sprinkle liberally with salt and allow to cool.

Place the eschalots and the remaining oil in a large pan and sauté on medium heat for 3–4 minutes. Once they soften up, add the ginger and garlic and cook on low heat for another 5 minutes. Add the miso paste, dashi, mirin, soy sauce, caster sugar and sake and stir well to combine. Cook for a couple of minutes until the mixture thickens slightly. Finally, add the roasted eggplant to the miso sauce and combine well.

Meanwhile, in a pot of salted boiling water, cook the soba noodles according to packet instructions (soba noodles usually require only 5–6 minutes of cooking). Drain the noodles and refresh slightly in cold water.

Combine the soba noodles, miso eggplant and Chinese shallots and season well. Place on a serving plate and scatter over the walnuts.

SERVES 4-6

4 eggplants (1.5 kg)
6 tbsp extra virgin olive oil
Sea salt and black pepper
200 g eschalots (about 6) (see note page 28), thinly sliced
2 tbsp chopped ginger
2 garlic cloves, crushed
3 tbsp mild miso paste
200 ml dashi (Japanese soup stock) or other vegetable stock
3 tbsp mirin
2 tbsp soy sauce
1 tbsp caster sugar
1 tbsp sake
400 g soba noodles
½ cup Chinese shallots (see note page 28), finely chopped
1 cup walnuts, lightly toasted and roughly chopped

ROASTED EGGPLANT WITH SOFRITO, CHICKPEAS AND ALMONDS

Over the years, I've tried many versions of sofrito, which is a slow-cooked Spanish sauce used as a base for many dishes, including stews and paella. But this sofrito recipe, adapted from the wonderful cookbook Movida *by Frank Camorra, is my favourite. It is a rich, intense, jam-like sauce that is cooked for almost two hours! Two hours may seem like a marathon, but you don't have to stand over it; just remember to stir it every now and then. The depth of flavour is mesmerising.*

Begin by making the sofrito. Heat the olive oil in a large frying pan over medium heat and add the onions, garlic, bay leaves and a big pinch of sea salt. Cook for about 10 minutes until the onions have softened. Add the capsicum and cook for 20 minutes, stirring occasionally. Reduce the heat to low, add the tomatoes and continue to cook uncovered for 1.5–2 hours, stirring every now and then, until you get a thick, jammy consistency. Check the seasoning and add some salt if required. This sofrito will keep in the fridge for 3 days, or you can freeze it.

Preheat the oven to 200°C.

Peel strips of skin from the eggplant, from top to bottom, so it leaves a stripy pattern. Cut the eggplant into 2 cm cubes and place on 2 large baking trays. Drizzle with the olive oil and roast for 25–30 minutes until soft and golden.

Combine the eggplant with the chickpeas, parsley and paprika. Stir through about 2 cups of the sofito sauce (you can freeze the rest of the sauce or use it for another recipe) and season with salt and pepper. To serve, scatter over the toasted almonds.

SERVES 4-6

4 eggplants (1.5 kg)
3 tbsp extra virgin olive oil
500 g cooked chickpeas (about 2 cans), drained
½ cup flat-leaf parsley leaves, roughly chopped
½ tsp smoked paprika
Sea salt and black pepper
¼ cup almonds, toasted and roughly chopped

SOFRITO (MAKES 3 CUPS)

125 ml extra virgin olive oil
2 brown onions, finely diced
2 garlic cloves, finely chopped
3 bay leaves
Sea salt
4 large red capsicums, deseeded and finely diced
250 g peeled tomatoes (drained weight of 1 can)

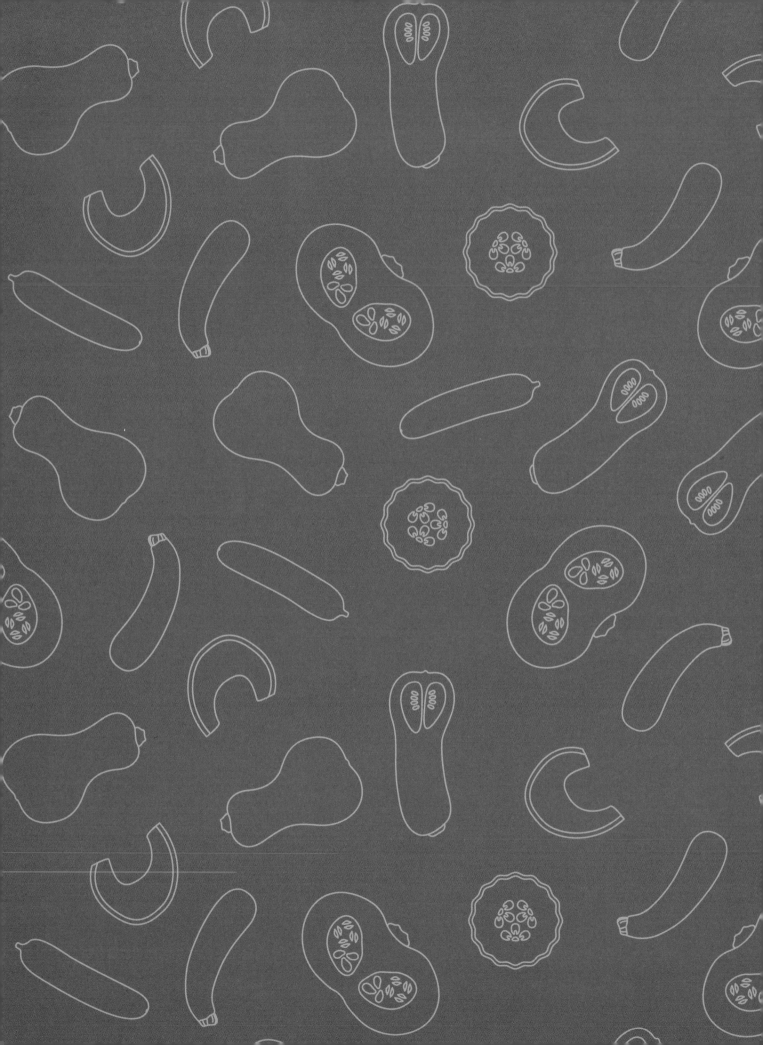

MEET THE MARROWS

PUMPKIN, ZUCCHINI, CUCUMBERS

PUMPKIN WITH CHICKPEAS, TOASTED COCONUT AND LEMON TAHINI

While holidaying in the Yasawa Islands of Fiji a few years back, I lived on this tropical-style pumpkin salad. Like much of Fijian cuisine, it's a real fusion dish, with warm toasted coconut and Asian snake beans brought to life by the vibrancy of kaffir lime leaves and a lemony tahini dressing. If snake beans are not in season, use green beans. Perfect for eating near a beach, perhaps lying in a hammock …

Preheat the oven to 200°C.

Toss the pumpkin in 2 tablespoons of the olive oil, season with salt and pepper and lay out evenly on a baking tray. Roast for 25 minutes, or until tender and slightly caramelised around the edges. Set aside to cool.

In a dry frying pan over medium heat, toast the shredded coconut, moving it around constantly until it has slightly browned. Remove the coconut from the pan immediately to stop further browning.

Make the lemon tahini by mixing the tahini, lemon juice and zest, garlic, oil and a pinch of salt and pepper. Add just enough water to thin the lemon tahini to the consistency of runny yoghurt.

In a wok or frying pan over high heat, add the remaining oil and fry the beans for 2 minutes until just tender. Allow to cool.

Combine the pumpkin with the chickpeas, beans, bean sprouts, toasted coconut, basil and kaffir lime leaves. Pour over the lemon tahini, scatter over the pumpkin and sesame seeds and top with coriander leaves.

SERVES 4-6

1 large butternut pumpkin (1 kg), peeled and cut into 2 cm cubes
3 tbsp extra virgin olive oil
Sea salt and black pepper
1 cup shredded coconut
200 g snake beans (or green beans), trimmed and cut into 3 cm pieces
500 g cooked chickpeas (about 2 cans), drained
200 g bean sprouts
½ cup Thai basil leaves (or regular basil leaves), torn
5 kaffir lime leaves, very thinly sliced
2 tbsp pumpkin seeds, toasted
2 tbsp sesame seeds, toasted
1 cup coriander leaves

LEMON TAHINI

1 cup tahini
Juice and zest of 1 lemon
1 garlic clove, crushed
4 tbsp extra virgin olive oil
Sea salt and black pepper

PUMPKIN WITH BURNT BUTTER, POPPY SEEDS AND CRISPY SAGE

This simple salad is inspired by the deep, rich flavours of one of my favourite Italian pasta dishes, pumpkin tortelli, which is traditionally served with burnt butter, toasted poppy seeds and crispy sage. The addition of a little grated nutmeg makes the pumpkin even sweeter and more intense. Add some rocket leaves or baby spinach if you desire. This is a perfect warming salad for cooler days.

Preheat the oven to 200°C.

Halve each pumpkin and cut into 1 cm wedges. Arrange on 2 large baking trays, drizzle over 2 tablespoons of the olive oil and sprinkle over the nutmeg, garlic, salt and pepper. Toss until the pumpkin is well coated. Roast for 25–30 minutes or until tender and starting to brown around the edges. Remove from the oven and allow to cool.

Melt the butter in a frying pan over medium heat. Once it starts to froth, add the sage leaves with a pinch of salt and stir in the poppy seeds. Turn the heat down to low and continue to fry for 1 minute until the sage becomes crispy and the butter browns.

Arrange the pumpkin wedges on a plate and spoon over the hot poppy seeds, crispy sage and burnt butter. Sprinkle over the feta and walnuts. Finish with a pinch of salt and pepper and drizzle over the remaining olive oil.

SERVES 4-6

2 butternut pumpkins (about 2 kg), peeled
3 tbsp extra virgin olive oil
1 tsp freshly grated (or ground) nutmeg
2 garlic cloves, finely chopped
Sea salt and black pepper
80 g butter
½ cup sage leaves, washed and dried
2 tbsp poppy seeds
200 g feta, crumbled
1 cup walnuts, lightly toasted and roughly chopped

CINNAMON PUMPKIN WITH CHICKPEAS, TAHINI AND CANDIED PUMPKIN SEEDS

For me, the thought of warm, spiced pumpkin always conjures up images of flickering jack-o'-lanterns and American holidays. This salad is inspired foremost by the classic Thanksgiving pumpkin pie, but is given a cheeky Middle Eastern twist with a nutty tahini sauce. The sweet, crunchy candied pumpkin seeds deliver an indulgent trick-or-treat surprise.

Preheat the oven to 220°C.

Toss the pumpkin and onions with the olive oil, cinnamon, ginger, salt and black pepper. Spread on a large baking tray and roast for 40 minutes or until golden. The red onion may cook faster than the pumpkin, so you may need to remove it before the pumpkin is cooked.

To make the candied pumpkin seeds, mix all the ingredients in a bowl. Spread the mixture in a single layer on a tray lined with baking paper. Bake until the pumpkin seeds are golden and slightly puffed (this will take about 10–12 minutes). Remove from the oven and season with more salt. Stir gently, leaving some clumps. Let cool completely and store in an airtight jar.

Whisk together the tahini, yoghurt, lemon juice, garlic and a good pinch of salt. Add water slowly until you have a smooth, creamy sauce. You want the consistency of double cream.

Combine the pumpkin with the chickpeas and parsley and toss gently. Transfer to a serving plate and spoon over the tahini sauce. To serve, scatter over the candied pumpkin seeds.

SERVES 4-6

1 large butternut pumpkin (1 kg), peeled and cut into 2 cm cubes
1 red onion, cut into 5 mm wedges
2–3 tbsp extra virgin olive oil
2 tsp ground cinnamon
1 tsp ground ginger
Sea salt and black pepper
4 tbsp tahini paste
3 tbsp Greek yoghurt
Juice of ½ lemon
1 small garlic clove, crushed
4 tbsp water
500 g cooked chickpeas (about 2 cans), drained
½ cup flat-leaf parsley leaves, roughly chopped

CANDIED PUMPKIN SEEDS

1 cup pumpkin seeds
3 tbsp sugar
1 large egg white, beaten
¼ tsp ground allspice
¼ tsp cayenne pepper
Pinch of coarse sea salt

BARBECUED CORN AND ROASTED BUTTERNUT PUMPKIN
WITH BLACK BEANS AND JALAPEÑO SOUR CREAM

This salad is inspired by the sublime corn dish at Cuban joint Café Habana in NoLiTa, NYC. Their barbecued corn is other-worldly, smothered in cheese, lime and chilli powder – it is definitely a dish I'd traverse the globe to eat. For this salad, substitute sweet potato for the butternut pumpkin if you prefer.

Preheat the oven to 200°C.

Place the pumpkin on a large baking tray, coat in 2–3 tablespoons of the olive oil and season well with salt and pepper. Bake for 25–30 minutes or until tender. Set aside to cool slightly.

Heat a griddle pan or barbecue to high. Drizzle the remaining olive oil over the corn and place on the pan or barbecue, turning it every minute or so to ensure that all sides are slightly blackened. When all the corn has been cooked, run a sharp knife down each side to remove the kernels. Add the paprika and a pinch of salt and pepper to the corn and toss well.

To make the cumin vinaigrette, whisk together all the ingredients and set aside.

To make the jalapeño sour cream, combine the ingredients and set aside.

Combine the pumpkin, black beans and corn and pour over the cumin vinaigrette. Toss well. To serve, spoon the salad onto a large plate, top with a few dollops of the jalapeño sour cream and scatter over the pumpkin seeds, coriander leaves and grated manchego cheese. Serve with lime wedges.

SERVES 4-6

1 butternut pumpkin (1 kg), peeled and cut into 2 cm cubes
3–4 tbsp extra virgin olive oil
Sea salt and black pepper
5 corn cobs, husks removed
1 tsp paprika
500 g cooked black beans, drained (about 2 cans)
½ cup pumpkin seeds, toasted
½ cup coriander leaves
50 g manchego cheese, grated
1 lime, quartered into wedges

CUMIN VINAIGRETTE

1 garlic clove, grated
1 tsp Dijon mustard
2 tsp white wine vinegar
2 tsp ground cumin
5 tbsp extra virgin olive oil
¼ cup coriander leaves

JALAPEÑO SOUR CREAM

300 ml sour cream
1 jalapeño chilli, deseeded and finely chopped

FRIED ZUCCHINI WITH GREEN COUSCOUS

One of the things I love most about vegetables is their vibrant natural colour. This salad seeks to bring a touch of lushness to your dining table. Use whatever soft herbs you have in your fridge or garden to make the green herb paste. A beautiful warm weather dish when the zucchinis are young and tender.

Preheat the oven to 120°C.

For the green herb paste, add the herbs, chilli, salt and garlic to the bowl of a food processor and pulse until finely chopped. Add the olive oil in a smooth stream and continue to whiz until you have a smooth paste.

Place the couscous in a shallow bowl along with the olive oil. Add the vegetable stock to the boiling water, pour over the couscous and stir well. Cover the bowl with cling wrap and let stand for 10 minutes. Uncover and dot the couscous with butter, cover with foil and heat in the oven for 5 minutes. Remove from the oven and fluff up the grains with a fork. Pour over the green herb paste and continue to fluff, working the paste well through the grains.

Heat 1 tablespoon of the sunflower oil in a large frying pan. Add the zucchini slices in a single layer and shallow-fry until golden brown on both sides. Transfer to a colander to drain. When all the zucchini slices have been cooked, tip them into a bowl, pour over the red wine vinegar and season well with a few big pinches of salt and pepper.

In a small frying pan, heat the remaining sunflower oil and add the spring onions. Cook until softened and then add the sugar and some salt. Cook for a further 2 minutes or until the onions are golden and sweet.

To serve, add the spring onions and rocket to the couscous and gently mix with a wooden spoon. Lay the zucchini over the couscous and scatter over the pistachios.

SERVES 4-6

400 g couscous

1 tbsp extra virgin olive oil

2 tsp vegetable stock powder

600 ml boiling water

30 g butter, cubed

2 tbsp sunflower oil

6 zucchini, cut lengthways into
  5 mm slices

3 tsp red wine vinegar

Sea salt and black pepper

5 spring onions (see note
  page 28), finely sliced

½ tsp caster sugar

2 cups (200 g) rocket leaves

¾ cup pistachio nuts, toasted
  and roughly chopped

GREEN HERB PASTE

2 cups soft herbs (any
  combination of parsley,
  mint, coriander, dill etc)

1 long green chilli, roughly
  chopped

1 tsp sea salt

1 garlic clove, crushed

100 ml extra virgin olive oil

CHARGRILLED ZUCCHINI AND PEARL BARLEY WITH WHIPPED FETA AND DILL

Zucchini and dill are a formidable duo. In this salad, the fennel–anise undertones of dill react perfectly with the subtle smokiness of charred zucchini, against the audacious backdrop of an effervescent whipped feta dressing. This creamy, salty, lemony sauce also makes a great dip.

In a large pot of water, add the pearl barley and a big pinch of salt. Bring to the boil and simmer for 25–30 minutes until the barley is swollen and tender (it should retain a chewy bite). Drain.

Heat a griddle pan or barbecue to high. Drizzle the olive oil over the zucchini and toss gently. Lay the zucchini slices on the pan or barbecue and cook for 2 minutes on each side until they are golden with nice char marks. Remove and place in a colander. Sprinkle with salt and pepper and toss with red wine vinegar. Continue until all the zucchini slices are cooked. Once cool enough to handle, you may need to cut the zucchini slices into smaller pieces, ideally about 5 cm long.

To prepare the whipped feta, blitz the feta, lemon juice and garlic in a food processor until smooth. With the motor running, add the oil in a thin stream and process until emulsified. Give the mixture a stir. Turn the motor back on and slowly add just enough water to get a nice creamy sauce, with the consistency of thick yoghurt. Season with a good amount of black pepper.

To serve, combine the zucchini with the pearl barley and dill. Stir through the whipped feta and top with the almonds.

SERVES 4-6

400 g pearl barley, rinsed
Sea salt and black pepper
2 tbsp extra virgin olive oil
10 zucchini (1 kg), cut
    lengthways into 5 mm slices
2 tbsp red wine vinegar
½ cup finely chopped dill fronds
¼ cup slivered almonds, toasted

WHIPPED FETA

300 g soft feta (Danish feta
    works best)
3 tsp lemon juice
1 garlic clove, grated
6 tbsp extra virgin olive oil
Black pepper

ZUCCHINI NOODLES WITH ASPARAGUS, FETA AND MINT

Raw zucchini is full of surprises. With its fleshy meat and texture, it is easily dressed up into a smashing salad. When choosing zucchini, go for medium or small sizes as the larger ones can be watery or bitter. This salad is of the 'no cooking required' variety, with the salty feta, lemon dressing and crunchy almonds effortlessly taking the zucchini to a very exciting place.

To make the dressing, combine the lemon, oil and garlic and whisk together until well combined. Add a good pinch of salt and pepper. Adjust the oil and lemon to achieve a balanced, tangy dressing.

Next, prepare the zucchini noodles. Using a julienne peeler, the julienne attachment on your mandolin or food processor, or just a simple box grater, shred the zucchini into long strips. Place in a colander, add a large pinch of salt and allow to sit for 20 minutes or so. This will draw out any excess moisture.

Using a sharp knife or peeler, finely slice the asparagus into thin strips.

Combine the zucchini noodles, asparagus, spring onions and herbs and stir through the lemon dressing. Crumble over the feta and serve topped with the almonds.

SERVES 4-6

8 zucchini (1.2 kg)
Sea salt
150 g (1 bunch) asparagus, trimmed and halved
2 spring onion bulbs (see note page 28), very thinly sliced
1 cup mint leaves
1 cup flat-leaf parsley leaves, roughly chopped
200 g Greek feta, crumbled
¼ cup slivered almonds, toasted

LEMON DRESSING

Juice of 1 lemon
½ cup extra virgin olive oil
1 garlic clove, grated
Sea salt and black pepper

CUCUMBER AND TOMATOES WITH HALOUMI AND TZATZIKI

This haloumi dish is one of our family dinner staples – it's a sure-fire crowd pleaser. The homemade tzatziki is creamy and made ever-so-slightly sweet with a dash of honey. I love the slice of bread at the bottom of the salad pile that becomes deliciously soggy from soaking up all the juices.

To make the tzatziki, add a pinch of salt to the cucumber and leave to drain in a sieve for 10 minutes. Every couple of minutes, push the cucumber down into the sieve to draw out extra moisture. Combine the drained cucumber with the remaining ingredients and stir together. Season well with a little salt and lots of black pepper.

Combine the tomato, cucumber, olives, garlic and oregano and mint leaves in a bowl and add 2 tablespoons olive oil and the red wine vinegar. Season well with salt and pepper and set aside.

Slice the haloumi into 5 mm-thick pieces. In a frying pan over medium heat, add 1 tablespoon of olive oil and fry the haloumi on each side for 1 minute or so, or until golden. Continue until all the haloumi has been cooked.

Arrange the slices of bread on a large platter or serving board. Pile the tomato and cucumber mixture on top of the bread, followed by the haloumi slices, then spoon over a few big dollops of tzatziki. Finish with a drizzle of olive oil and lots of cracked black pepper.

SERVES 4-6

6 roma tomatoes (500 g), cut into 1 cm dice
4 Lebanese cucumbers (1 kg), cut into 1 cm dice
½ cup kalamata olives, pitted and roughly chopped
1 small garlic clove, crushed
1 tbsp oregano leaves
¼ cup mint leaves, torn
4 tbsp extra virgin olive oil
1 tsp red wine vinegar
Sea salt and black pepper
500 g haloumi
4–6 slices of sourdough (or other crusty bread

TZATZIKI

Sea salt and black pepper
2 Lebanese cucumbers (500 g), finely grated
300 g Greek yoghurt
1 tsp dried mint
1 garlic clove, crushed
1 tbsp extra virgin olive oil
1 tsp honey

IN THE MOOD FOR ASIAN

NOODLES, SEAWEED, GINGER, TOFU, ASIAN GREENS

NASI GORENG WITH ASIAN GREENS

In Bali, nasi goreng is found at every warung and roadside food cart. Which is perfect, as it's a very addictive dish. Buoyed by eye-opening food experiences in Bali, this is my own version of this iconic fried rice dish, with a signature Arthur Street Kitchen tweak and twist. Use seasonal greens.

For the spice paste, blend all of the ingredients in a food processor until you have a smooth paste.

For the egg omelette strips, beat the eggs and season with a pinch of salt and pepper. Heat the oil in a small frying pan and swirl to cover the pan. Pour in enough egg to form a thin layer over the base of the pan. Cook on low heat until the egg has almost set on top. Flip it over and cook for a few seconds. Let cool and then roll up the egg and cut it into long 5 mm strips. Repeat the process with the remaining egg.

Heat a wok or large frying pan until smoking hot. Add the spice paste and stir-fry for 1–2 minutes. Add the soy sauce, tomato puree, kecap manis and the rice and continue to stir-fry for a further few minutes until everything is heated through. Add the greens and stir-fry for 2 minutes or until the greens are just tender yet still crisp. Take the wok off the heat, then fold through the bean sprouts and shallots.

Serve the fried rice topped with the egg and cucumber rounds. Add a scattering of crispy fried shallots and serve the crushed peanuts on the side.

SERVES 4-6

3 large free-range eggs
Sea salt and black pepper
2 tbsp vegetable oil
2 tbsp soy sauce
2 tbsp tomato puree
2 tbsp kecap manis
3–4 cups brown rice, chilled
1 bunch (350 g) choy sum (or other Asian greens), stems and leaves trimmed and cut into 5 cm pieces
2 cups (100 g) bean sprouts
½ cup Chinese shallots (see note page 28), finely sliced
1 Lebanese cucumber, peeled and sliced into thin rounds
¼ cup crispy fried shallots
¼ cup roasted peanuts, crushed

SPICE PASTE

3–4 tbsp vegetable oil
2 garlic cloves
3 eschalots (see note page 28), roughly chopped
1 long red chilli, roughly chopped
Sea salt

SEAWEED WITH SESAME, TOFU AND MUNG BEAN VERMICELLI

The aisles of the Asian supermarket hold such exciting possibilities for the salad enthusiast. While I didn't eat a lot of Chinese salads growing up, nowadays I find the heady, uncompromising flavours of Asian cuisine perfect for salads. It was my mum, the best instinctive cook I know, who one day presented me with a bag of dried seaweed threads and demanded (in Cantonese), 'Here, make a salad out of this!' Ever the obedient Chinese daughter, I did just that. Here it is.

To make the sesame dressing, combine all the ingredients and mix well. Taste and adjust the oil, vinegars and sugar until you get the right balance.

Prepare the seaweed by soaking it a large bowl of hot tap water. Allow the seaweed to soak for 10 minutes and then rinse really well under cold running water.

Soak the mung bean vermicelli in boiling water for about 5 minutes and then drain.

Bring a pot of water to the boil, add a big pinch of salt and blanch the vermicelli for 1 minute. Remove the vermicelli with tongs and drain in a colander, refreshing under cold running water. In the same pot of water, add the seaweed and also blanch for just 1 minute. Drain and rinse well.

Combine the seaweed, vermicelli, tofu, chilli, bean sprouts and shallots with the sesame dressing and toss well. To serve, top with the sesame seeds.

SERVES 4-6

100 g dried seaweed threads
  (or other dried seaweed)
200 g mung bean vermicelli
Sea salt
220 g (1 packet) five-spice tofu,
  thinly sliced
1 long red chilli, deseeded and
  finely chopped
200 g bean sprouts, washed
  and drained
½ cup Chinese shallots (see
  note page 28), finely sliced
¼ cup sesame seeds, toasted

SESAME DRESSING

2 tbsp sesame oil
1 tbsp mirin
1 tbsp rice wine vinegar
1 tbsp tamari
1 tsp brown sugar
Sea salt and black pepper

SOBA NOODLES WITH SHREDDED VEGETABLES AND GINGER–SHALLOT SAUCE

Soba noodles are a great ingredient to keep in your pantry for those 'I don't know what to eat' days. Here, I've teamed soba noodles with my childhood food fantasy – ginger–shallot sauce. Conveniently, this ginger–shallot recipe makes about 1 litre – keep leftovers in the fridge to enjoy over plain rice, omelette or even Hainanese chicken rice! Eat this salad chilled, if you prefer.

To make the dressing, first mince the ginger. If you prefer the ginger very fine, simply run the root over a microplane. If you prefer the ginger slightly chunkier (which is how I've always eaten it), chop with a knife.

Combine the ginger, shallots, salt, vinegar and soy in a bowl. Heat the oil over medium heat until it starts to boil. Take off the heat immediately and add it to the ginger–shallot mix, taking care not to burn yourself, as the oil will spit when it makes contact with the ginger–shallot mix. Allow to cool.

Bring a large pot of salted water to the boil, add the soba noodles and cook for 4–5 minutes or until just tender. Drain and refresh under cold running water.

Using a mandolin, food processor or knife, shred the cabbage finely and grate the carrot into long strips. Add the vegetables and shallots to the soba noodles and pour over 1 cup (or more) of ginger–shallot sauce. Toss well to combine. Transfer the salad to a large platter, season well and sprinkle over the toasted sesame seeds.

SERVES 4-6

Sea salt and black pepper
500 g soba noodles
500 g purple (or white) cabbage
5 carrots (500 g), peeled
½ cup Chinese shallots (see note page 28), finely sliced
½ cup sesame seeds, toasted

GINGER–SHALLOT SAUCE

150 g ginger, peeled
150 g Chinese shallots (see note page 28), finely sliced
2 tsp sea salt
1 tbsp rice wine vinegar
1 tbsp soy sauce
1 cup rice bran oil (or other neutral oil, such as grapeseed)

HOT AND SOUR MUNG BEAN VERMICELLI
WITH MUSHROOMS, WOMBOK AND TOFU

This salad is inspired by Thai tom yum soup. With its intoxicating blend of spice and sourness, this light yet nourishing salad will awaken dormant tastebuds with its heavy hit of ginger, chilli, lemongrass and coriander. Use any noodles you like. A real knockout dish, in more ways than one.

Start by making the spice paste for the hot and sour dressing. In a food processor, blitz together the eschalots, garlic, ginger, chilli (remove the seeds if you don't want it too hot), lemongrass, kaffir lime leaves and coriander. Add the tomatoes and a pinch of salt and blitz again until you achieve a smooth paste.

Place the spice paste and water in a medium-sized pot and bring to the boil. Reduce the heat and simmer for 20 minutes. Remove from the heat and add the lime juice, soy sauce and sugar. Stir until the sugar has dissolved. Taste for a balance of flavours, adjusting if required.

Soak the mung bean vermicelli in warm water. Allow to soften for about 15 minutes. Drain.

Bring a large pot of water to the boil and add a big pinch of salt and the green beans. Cook for 4–5 minutes until tender but still crisp. Just before the beans are ready, add the mung bean vermicelli and cook for about 1 minute. Drain both the beans and vermicelli and refresh immediately under cold running water.

Combine the mushrooms, vermicelli, tofu puffs, beans, wombok and herbs with the hot and sour dressing. Serve with a scatter of crispy fried shallots over the top.

SERVES 4-6

100 g mung bean vermicelli
Sea salt
200 g green beans, trimmed and cut into 5 cm pieces
200 g button mushrooms, finely sliced
150 g tofu puffs, halved in triangles
300 g wombok, shredded
½ cup Vietnamese mint leaves
½ cup Thai basil leaves
½ cup coriander leaves
¼ cup crispy fried shallots

HOT AND SOUR DRESSING

3 eschalots (see note page 28), roughly chopped
2 garlic cloves, roughly chopped
3 cm piece of ginger, peeled and chopped
1–2 red bird's eye chillies
3 stalks lemongrass (white end only), finely sliced
3 kaffir lime leaves, finely sliced
½ cup coriander roots and stem
2 tomatoes, chopped
Sea salt
Juice of 1 lime
2 tbsp soy sauce
2–3 tbsp shaved palm sugar

MIE GORENG WITH ASIAN GREENS

One of the joys of travelling is the discovery of authentic new flavours and traditional cooking techniques. In Bali, it was an honour to watch the locals prepare simple, delicious dishes with such finesse, using the most basic ingredients. The noodles in Bali are plain to the eye but the palate tells a very different story – they are packed with a sweet spiciness that is intense yet clean. For my version of mie goreng, it is the spice paste that delivers such character to an otherwise simple dish.

To prepare the spice paste, using a mortar and pestle, add the garlic, eschalots, peppercorns, chilli and a good pinch of sea salt. Pound the ingredients together until you get a fine paste. Alternatively, use a food processor to blitz together.

For this recipe, you can use whatever noodles you like. Thick rice noodles also work well. Bring a pot of water to the boil, add a big pinch of salt and cook the noodles (according to the packet instructions) until just al dente. Do not overcook the noodles as you don't want them to get mushy when fried.

In a wok or large frying pan over high heat, add 1–2 tablespoons of oil. Add the spice paste and stir-fry for 1–2 minutes or until you can smell the aroma. Add the wombok and greens and toss well to make sure the paste is evenly distributed. Add the vegetable stock, noodles and kecap manis and toss for another minute or so. Remove from the heat and add the bean sprouts and Chinese shallots. Toss well to combine and season with sea salt and white pepper.

To serve, top with crispy fried shallots.

SERVES 4-6

500 g fresh egg noodles (or thick rice noodles)
Sea salt and white pepper
1–2 tbsp vegetable oil
500 g wombok, shredded
1 bunch (350 g) choy sum or other Asian greens, cut into 5 cm pieces
½ cup liquid vegetable stock
3 tbsp kecap manis
200 g bean sprouts
1 cup Chinese shallots (see note page 28), finely sliced
¼ cup crispy fried shallots

SPICE PASTE

1 garlic clove
4 eschalots (see note page 28)
½ tsp whole white peppercorns
1 red bird's eye chilli, deseeded if you prefer it less hot
1 tsp sea salt

LAKSA HOKKIEN NOODLES
WITH GREEN BEANS, CHINESE BROCCOLI AND TOFU

For me, laksa soup is one of those meals I often crave. This salad transforms the heady, complex aromas of laksa into a punchy, flavour-packed salad. Don't be put off by the list of ingredients – I promise, the flavour is really worth the effort! Plus, it's a wonderfully cathartic experience to make your own curry paste. If you are short on time, substitute with a store-bought paste.

To make the laksa sauce, place the eschalots, garlic, ginger, lemongrass, ground coriander, red chilli flakes and sambal oelek in a food processor. Add 3 tablespoons of the vegetable oil and the coriander stems and process into a smooth paste. Heat the remaining oil in a saucepan and fry the laksa paste over low heat for 15 minutes, stirring often to prevent burning. Add the vegetable stock, curry leaves, curry powder, salt, sugar and coconut milk and simmer gently for 20 minutes. Taste and add more salt or sugar if needed.

Prepare the vegetables by trimming the Asian greens into 5 cm pieces. Trim the green beans and cut into pieces about the same length as the greens. Halve the tofu puffs into triangles.

In a pot of salted boiling water, blanch the beans for 4–5 minutes. Just before the beans are ready, add the greens to the pan and blanch for 1–2 minutes until just tender. Remove the beans and greens with tongs and refresh immediately under cold running water. In the same pot of boiling water, add the hokkien noodles and cook for 2–3 minutes or until just tender. Drain and refresh under cold water.

Combine the noodles, greens, beans, bean sprouts and tofu puffs with the laksa dressing and toss until everything is well coated. Sprinkle over the coriander leaves and serve the lime wedges on the side.

SERVES 4-6

1 bunch (400 g) Chinese broccoli or other Asian greens
200 g green beans
150 g fried tofu puffs
Sea salt
500 g hokkien noodles
200 g bean sprouts
½ cup coriander leaves
1 lime, cut into wedges

LAKSA SAUCE

12 eschalots (400 g) (see note page 28), peeled
3 garlic cloves, peeled
2 cm piece of ginger, peeled
2 stalks lemongrass (soft white stem only), sliced
3 tsp ground coriander
1 tsp dried red chilli flakes
1 tbsp sambal oelek
4 tbsp vegetable oil
1 cup coriander stems
500 ml liquid vegetable stock
8 curry leaves
1 tbsp curry powder
2 tsp salt
2 tbsp caster sugar
400 ml coconut milk

SPICED COCONUT WITH BLANCHED VEGETABLES

Childhood memories of Coconut Roughs and Summer Rolls have left me with a strong adoration for coconut. This salad focuses squarely on this beautifully exotic fruit. It is a version of urap, an Indonesian vegetable salad with a coconut dressing. It's traditionally made with fresh coconut, but store-bought shredded coconut works just fine. Blanched veggies have never tasted so good!

For the spiced shredded coconut, blend the chillies, garlic, eschalots and ginger in a food processor to form a smooth paste. If the mixture is too thick, add a splash of water and pulse again to bring everything together. In another bowl, make a sugar syrup by combining the tamarind, palm sugar and water and stir until the sugar has dissolved.

In a wok or large frying pan, heat the oil and stir-fry the spice paste with the kaffir lime leaves for 5 minutes or until slightly browned. Next, add the sugar syrup to the paste and cook until the mixture boils. Add the shredded coconut and a pinch of salt and stir well to combine. Turn the heat down to low and stir frequently until the coconut has soaked up all the liquid and is almost dry. Store this mixture in an airtight container in the fridge for up to 5 days.

Bring a large pot of water to the boil and add some salt. Blanch the green beans for about 4–5 minutes until tender. Just before the beans are done, add the Asian greens, wombok and bean sprouts and blanch for just 1–2 minutes until tender but still crisp. Drain and refresh immediately under cold running water.

Combine the blanched vegetables with the five-spice tofu and stir through the spiced coconut. Season and serve with crispy fried shallots and cucumber rounds on the side.

SERVES 4-6

Sea salt and black pepper
200 g green beans, trimmed
and halved
2 bunches (700 g) Asian greens
(Chinese broccoli, choy sum
or bok choy), trimmed into
5 cm pieces
700 g wombok, shredded
200 g bean sprouts
220 g (1 packet) five-spice tofu,
thinly sliced
¼ cup crispy fried shallots
2 Lebanese cucumbers, peeled
and sliced into rounds

SPICED SHREDDED COCONUT

2 red bird's eye chillies
3 garlic cloves
8 eschalots (see note page 28),
peeled
3 cm piece of ginger, peeled
2 tsp tamarind puree
2 tbsp palm sugar, shaved
2 cups hot water
2 tbsp vegetable oil
4 kaffir lime leaves, finely sliced
2 cups (250 g) shredded coconut
Sea salt

GADO GADO WITH SATE SAUCE

During a family sojourn to Bali, two beautiful local ladies taught us how we should all eat, no matter where we live in the world – treat every meal like a celebration by cooking together and eating together. This is exactly the ethos of this cookbook. In Bali, I learnt how the locals make and eat one of their signature dishes, gado gado – simple blanched vegetables with a very addictive sweet peanut sate.

To make the sate sauce, add the oil to a small frying pan and fry the chillies, eschalots and garlic for 5 minutes or until softened. In a food processor or blender, add the eschalot mixture along with the peanuts, kecap manis, palm sugar and salt and blitz to combine. With the motor running, slowly add the hot water until you have a smooth sauce. This sauce can be stored in a jar in the refrigerator for up to 7 days.

Season the tofu well with salt and pepper. Heat the oil in a large frying pan over medium heat. Add the tofu slices to the pan and fry for 2 minutes on each side until golden brown. When cool, cut into thin strips.

Peel the potatoes and chop them into bite-sized pieces. In a pot of salted boiling water, boil the potatoes for 8–10 minutes or until just tender.

Bring a large pot of water to the boil and add a big pinch of salt. Add the choy sum, wombok and bean sprouts to the water and blanch for about 1–2 minutes or until just tender. Remove, refresh under cold running water and drain well.

Combine the blanched vegetables, potatoes, tofu, shallots and sesame oil. Top with the sate sauce. Serve with the boiled eggs on top and the cucumber slices and crispy fried shallots on the side.

SERVES 4-6

500 g firm tofu, cut into 5 mm slices
Sea salt and black pepper
1 tbsp vegetable oil
10 potatoes (700 g)
2 bunches choy sum (800 g), trimmed into 5 cm pieces
700 g wombok, finely sliced
250 g bean sprouts
4 Chinese shallots (see note page 28), finely sliced
1 tbsp sesame oil
4 boiled eggs, halved
2 Lebanese cucumbers, peeled and sliced into 2 mm rounds
½ cup crispy fried shallots

SATE SAUCE

2 tbsp vegetable oil
2 long red chillies, deseeded and sliced
5 eschalots (see note page 28)
3 garlic cloves, sliced
200 g roasted peanuts
4 tbsp kecap manis
2 tbsp palm or brown sugar
1 tsp sea salt
1 cup hot water

ACKNOWLEDGEMENTS

This book is for the people of Surry Hills – the 'locals' who like to eat salads. Thank you for the delightful repartee, for loving vegetables as much as me, and for allowing me to feed you. Thank you to my *community: my neighbourhood friends who, over coffee and conversation, bring such calm and joy to my daily life.*

The story of *Community* wasn't complete until, on one sunny autumnal Wednesday morning, a dark-haired lady came knocking on my door with her pocket-sized Poppy by her side. She smiled, I laughed and it was a done deal. When Luisa Brimble shoots her camera, magic is made. Her staggering talent is clear for all to see in this book. Thank you so much for bringing such warmth and sincerity to this book and into my life.

Then in breezed Erika Raxworthy, who, with her creative soul, free-spirited nonchalance and razor-sharp eye, styled the photographs with such spunk. Thank you for being amazing.

Thank you to my friend and art director Martha Zakarya. You are a wunderkind, an old soul with a sparkling mind who has brought such a beautiful, understated style to this book. Somehow you always manage to capture what I'm thinking before I've even thought it.

Thank you to Monica Pen for jumping on board at the eleventh hour and for dazzling me with your cool, clean line work. You're a big talent, waiting for take-off. Thank you to Amanda Lee Denning for bringing my water-colour dreams to life.

Thank you to all my friends and neighbours who loaned me props, dishes and often their hands for the photo shoot: Gabi Wynhausen, Renee Bull, Nike and Chris at Collector Store, Davida Sweeney, Vanessa Trowell, Keith Muggeridge-Breene, and Cristina Caicedo. Thank you to all the community salad eaters who appear in this book.

I want to thank Amy Low and Matt, Wei, Doug and Irma at Incu for their friendship, laughter and for being such an important part of Arthur Street Kitchen from day one; Caroline, Sophie and Jane at *Broadsheet* for their continued support and kind words; and Tokyo Bike for helping me out of a bike pickle more than once. Thanks to my dear friends Lee and Remy for allowing me to use their café as my office in the early days, for plying me with great coffee and for giving me my start in selling food (Surry Hills still misses you…).

Thank you to my husband Ross, a man of interminable patience, who has been my collaborator for what seems like forever (in a good way!). He is the perfect guy to have around when pursuing a caper, and, as far as capers go, this book has been one of our greatest. Our other great caper has been parenthood. Thank you to my triumvirate, my three favourite mini-people, Scout, Dash and Huck, who bring their very own special brand of happy chaos into our lives.

Lastly, thank you to my mum – the best cook I know – for showing me the absolute joy of cooking for your family. She is the master and I am her apprentice.

HM

ALMONDS

59 moroccan sweet potato, chickpeas and couscous with chermoula
65 chargrilled broccoli with chickpeas, almonds, lemon and chilli
81 balsamic brussels sprouts and puy lentils with parmesan and mint
105 mixed mushrooms with farro, feta and almonds
121 peas and mint with quinoa, feta and almonds
151 chargrilled zucchini and pearl barley with whipped feta and dill
137 roasted eggplant with sofrito, chickpeas and almonds

APPLES

97 thai kohlrabi and cabbage slaw with apple and crushed peanuts

ASPARAGUS

55 chargrilled fennel and asparagus with pearl couscous and coriander oil
153 zucchini noodles with asparagus, feta and mint

BABA GHANOUSH

79 smoky baba ghanoush with roasted cauliflower, lentils and pomegranate

BALSAMIC VINEGAR

81 balsamic brussels sprouts and puy lentils with parmesan and mint
117 balsamic–roasted pears with lentils, gorgonzola and sage
119 puy lentils with balsamic–soaked figs, watercress and walnuts
131 slow-roasted balsamic tomatoes with spelt pasta, porcini and ricotta

BASIL

67 broccoli and orecchiette with yoghurt and peas
85 turnips, dutch carrots and cannellini beans with sunflower-seed pesto
91 cavolo nero and borlotti beans with tomatoes, croutons and basil cream
111 pearl barley with pistachios, rocket and basil oil
123 sugar snap peas, jerusalem artichokes, cannellini beans and orecchiette with warrigal green pesto
127 baked tomatoes with capers, olives and croutons
129 panzanella with heirloom tomatoes
131 slow-roasted balsamic tomatoes with spelt pasta, porcini and ricotta

BEANS, GREEN

141 pumpkin with chickpeas, toasted coconut and lemon tahini
165 hot and sour mung bean vermicelli with mushrooms, chinese cabbage and tofu
169 laksa hokkien noodles with green beans, chinese broccoli and tofu
171 spiced coconut with blanched vegetables
173 gado gado with sate sauce

BEAN SPROUTS

141 pumpkin with chickpeas, toasted coconut and lemon tahini
159 nasi goreng with asian greens
161 seaweed with sesame, tofu and mung bean vermicelli
167 mie goreng with asian greens
169 laksa hokkien noodles with green beans, chinese broccoli and tofu
171 spiced coconut with blanched vegetables
173 gado gado with sate sauce

BEETROOT

41 roasted beetroot with caramelised turnips, edamame and wasabi mayonnaise
43 pickled beetroot with puy lentils, baby spinach and cheddar
45 beetroot and dill with crème fraiche and walnuts
47 roasted beetroot, shaved fennel and broad beans with skordalia

BLACK BEANS

147 barbecued corn and roasted pumpkin with black beans and jalapeño sour cream

BLACK BEANS (CHINESE SALTED)

133 black bean eggplant with snake beans and brown rice

BLACK FUNGUS

101 black fungus and five-spice tofu with mung bean vermicelli

BLOOD ORANGES

49 za'atar–roasted carrots with kale, freekeh and blood orange–maple dressing

BORLOTTI BEANS

91 cavolo nero and borlotti beans with tomatoes, croutons and basil cream

BREAD

47 roasted beetroot, shaved fennel and broad beans with skordalia
73 roasted cauliflower with caper vinaigrette and lemon–parsley pangrattato
89 ribollita salad with kale, cavolo nero, fennel, tomatoes, cannellini beans and ciabatta
91 cavolo nero and borlotti beans with tomatoes, croutons and basil cream
103 pine mushrooms with eschalots, cherry tomatoes and sourdough croutons
127 baked tomatoes with capers, olives and croutons
129 panzanella with heirloom tomatoes

BROAD BEANS

47 roasted beetroot, shaved fennel and broad beans with skordalia

BROCCOLI

65 chargrilled broccoli with chickpeas, almonds, lemon and chilli
67 broccoli and orecchiette with yoghurt and peas
69 sweet sesame broccoli and edamame with quinoa
71 smashed chickpeas with broccoli and dukkah

BRUSSELS SPROUTS

81 balsamic brussels sprouts and puy lentils with parmesan and mint
83 chargrilled brussels sprouts with lotus root and sweet marinated tofu

BURNT BUTTER

143 pumpkin with burnt butter, poppy seeds and crispy sage

BUTTER BEANS

77 chargrilled cauliflower with fried butter beans and pumpkin hummus

CABBAGE

93 cabbage and fennel with peas, mint, parmesan and lemon

95 vietnamese cabbage salad with tofu, rice vermicelli and peanuts

97 thai kohlrabi and cabbage slaw with apple and crushed peanuts

163 soba noodles with shredded vegetables and ginger–shallot sauce

CANNELLINI BEANS

85 turnips, dutch carrots and cannellini beans with sunflower-seed pesto

89 ribollita salad with kale, cavolo nero, fennel, tomatoes, cannellini beans and ciabatta

123 sugar snap peas, jerusalem artichokes, cannellini beans and orecchiette with warrigal green pesto

CAPERS

65 chargrilled broccoli with chickpeas, almonds, lemon and chilli

73 roasted cauliflower with caper vinaigrette and lemon–parsley pangrattato

127 baked tomatoes with capers, olives and croutons

CAPSICUM

137 roasted eggplant with sofrito, chickpeas and almonds

CARROTS

49 za'atar–roasted carrots with kale, freekeh and blood orange–maple dressing

51 spiced roasted carrot with fennel and caramelised onion

53 honey–roasted carrots with mung beans and labneh

85 turnips, dutch carrots and cannellini beans with sunflower-seed pesto

95 vietnamese cabbage salad with tofu, rice vermicelli and peanuts

163 soba noodles with shredded vegetables and ginger–shallot sauce

CAULIFLOWER

73 roasted cauliflower with caper vinaigrette and lemon–parsley pangrattato

75 spiced persian red lentils with roasted cauliflower and yoghurt

77 chargrilled cauliflower with fried butter beans and pumpkin hummus

79 smoky baba ghanoush with roasted cauliflower, lentils and pomegranate

109 winter tabbouleh with quinoa, sumac cauliflower, pomegranate and feta

101 black fungus and five-spice tofu with mung bean vermicelli

CAVOLO NERO

89 ribollita salad with kale, cavolo nero, fennel, tomatoes, cannellini beans and ciabatta

91 cavolo nero and borlotti beans with tomato, croutons and basil cream

CHEDDAR

43 pickled beetroot with puy lentils, baby spinach and cheddar

CHICKPEAS

51 spiced roasted carrot with fennel and caramelised onion

59 moroccan sweet potato, chickpeas and couscous with chermoula

65 chargrilled broccoli with chickpeas, almonds, lemon and chilli

71 smashed chickpeas with broccoli and dukkah

137 roasted eggplant with sofrito, chickpeas and almonds

141 pumpkin with chickpeas, toasted coconut and lemon tahini

145 cinnamon pumpkin with chickpeas, tahini and candied pumpkin seeds

CHILLI

65 chargrilled broccoli with chickpeas, almonds, lemon and chilli

71 smashed chickpeas with broccoli and dukkah

83 chargrilled brussels sprouts with lotus root and sweet marinated tofu

95 vietnamese cabbage salad with tofu, rice vermicelli and peanuts

97 thai kohlrabi and cabbage slaw with apple and crushed peanuts

115 spicy fried edamame with eggplant and soba noodles

147 barbecued corn and roasted pumpkin with black beans and jalapeno sour cream

149 fried zucchini with green couscous

159 nasi goreng with asian greens

165 hot and sour mung bean vermicelli with mushrooms, chinese cabbage and tofu

167 mie goreng with asian greens

171 spiced coconut with blanched vegetables

CHINESE SHALLOTS

41 roasted beetroot with caramelised turnips, edamame and wasabi mayonnaise

109 winter tabbouleh with quinoa, sumac cauliflower, pomegranate and feta

133 black bean eggplant with snake beans and brown rice

163 soba noodles with shredded vegetables and ginger–shallot sauce

173 gado gado with sate sauce

CHOY SUM

159 nasi goreng with asian greens

167 mie goreng with asian greens

171 spiced coconut with blanched vegetables

173 gado gado with sate sauce

CINNAMON

145 cinnamon pumpkin with chickpeas, tahini and candied pumpkin seeds

COCONUT

141 pumpkin with chickpeas, toasted coconut and lemon tahini

171 spiced coconut with blanched vegetables

CORIANDER

55 chargrilled fennel and asparagus with pearl couscous and coriander oil

57 baked sweet potato with rocket, feta and black olive–walnut relish

59 moroccan sweet potato, chickpeas and couscous with chermoula

169 laksa hokkien noodles with green beans, chinese broccoli and tofu

CORN

147 barbecued corn and roasted pumpkin with black beans and jalapeño sour cream

COUSCOUS

59 moroccan sweet potato, chickpeas and couscous with chermoula

149 fried zucchini with green couscous

COUSCOUS, PEARL
55 chargrilled fennel and asparagus with pearl couscous and coriander oil

CRÈME FRAICHE
45 beetroot and dill with crème fraiche and walnuts
127 baked tomatoes with capers, olives and croutons

CROUTONS
91 cavolo nero and borlotti beans with tomatoes, croutons and basil cream
103 pine mushrooms with eschalots, cherry tomatoes and sourdough croutons
127 baked tomatoes with capers, olives and croutons
129 panzanella with heirloom tomatoes

CUCUMBER
155 cucumber and tomatoes with haloumi and tzatziki
159 nasi goreng with asian greens
171 spiced coconut with blanched vegetables
173 gado gado with sate sauce

DILL
45 beetroot and dill with crème fraiche and walnuts
49 za'atar–roasted carrots with kale, freekeh and blood orange–maple dressing
151 chargrilled zucchini and pearl barley with whipped feta and dill

DUKKAH
71 smashed chickpeas with broccoli and dukkah

EDAMAME
41 roasted beetroot with caramelised turnips, edamame and wasabi mayonnaise
69 sweet sesame broccoli and edamame with quinoa
115 spicy fried edamame with eggplant and soba noodles

EGGS
159 nasi goreng with asian greens
173 gado gado with sate sauce

EGGPLANT
79 smoky baba ghanoush with roasted cauliflower, lentils and pomegranate
115 spicy fried edamame with eggplant and soba noodles
133 black bean eggplant with snake beans and brown rice
135 miso eggplant with soba noodles and walnuts
137 roasted eggplant with sofrito, chickpeas and almonds

ESCHALOTS
43 pickled beetroot with puy lentils, baby spinach and cheddar
83 chargrilled brussels sprouts with lotus root and sweet marinated tofu
135 pine mushrooms with eschalots, cherry tomatoes and sourdough croutons
135 miso eggplant with soba noodles and walnuts
159 nasi goreng with asian greens

165 hot and sour mung bean vermicelli with mushrooms, chinese cabbage and tofu
167 mie goreng with asian greens
171 spiced coconut with blanched vegetables
173 gado gado with sate sauce

FARRO
105 mixed mushrooms with farro, feta and almonds

FENNEL
47 roasted beetroot, shaved fennel and broad beans with skordalia
51 spiced roasted carrots with fennel and caramelised onion
55 chargrilled fennel and asparagus with pearl couscous and coriander oil
89 ribollita salad with kale, cavolo nero, fennel, tomatoes, cannellini beans and ciabatta
93 cabbage and fennel with peas, mint, parmesan and lemon

FETA
51 spiced roasted carrots with fennel and caramelised onion
57 baked sweet potato with rocket, feta and black olive–walnut relish
105 mixed mushrooms with farro, feta and almonds
109 winter tabbouleh with quinoa, sumac cauliflower, pomegranate and feta
111 pearl barley with pistachios, rocket and basil oil
121 peas and mint with quinoa, feta and almonds
119 puy lentils with balsamic-soaked figs, watercress and walnuts
151 chargrilled zucchini and pearl barley with whipped feta and dill
153 zucchini noodles with asparagus, feta and mint

FIGS
119 puy lentils with balsamic-soaked figs, watercress and walnuts

FREEKEH
49 za'atar–roasted carrots with kale, freekeh and blood orange–maple dressing

GAI LARN (CHINESE BROCCOLI)
169 laksa hokkien noodles with green beans, chinese broccoli and tofu
171 spiced coconut with blanched vegetables

GINGER
87 ginger–peanut kale with tofu and quinoa
95 vietnamese cabbage salad with tofu, rice vermicelli and peanuts
97 thai kohlrabi and cabbage slaw with apple and crushed peanuts
115 spicy fried edamame with eggplant and soba noodles
133 black bean eggplant with snake beans and brown rice
163 soba noodles with shredded vegetables and ginger–shallot sauce
165 hot and sour mung bean vermicelli with mushrooms, chinese cabbage and tofu
169 laksa hokkien noodles with green beans, chinese broccoli and tofu
171 spiced coconut with blanched vegetables

GORGONZOLA
117 balsamic–roasted pears with lentils, gorgonzola and sage

HALOUMI
155 cucumber and tomato with haloumi and tzatziki

HAZELNUTS
49 za'atar–roasted carrots with kale, freekeh and blood orange–maple dressing
51 spiced roasted carrots with fennel and caramelised onion
71 smashed chickpeas with broccoli and dukkah

HONEY
53 honey–roasted carrots with mung beans and labneh
61 spiced sweet potato, puy lentils and rocket with honey walnuts
69 sweet sesame broccoli and edamame with quinoa

JERUSALEM ARTICHOKES
123 sugar snap peas, jerusalem artichokes, cannellini beans and orecchiette with warrigal green pesto

KAFFIR LIME LEAVES
141 pumpkin with chickpeas, toasted coconut and lemon tahini
165 hot and sour mung bean vermicelli with mushrooms, Chinese cabbage and tofu

KALE
49 za'atar–roasted carrots with kale, freekeh and blood orange–maple dressing
87 ginger–peanut kale with tofu and quinoa
89 ribollita salad with kale, cavolo nero, fennel, tomatoes, cannellini beans and ciabatta

KOHLRABI
97 thai kohlrabi and cabbage slaw with apple and crushed peanuts

LABNEH
53 honey–roasted carrots with mung beans and labneh

LEMONS
65 chargrilled broccoli with chickpeas, almonds, lemon and chilli
71 smashed chickpeas with broccoli and dukkah
73 roasted cauliflower with caper vinaigrette and lemon–parsley pangrattato
93 cabbage and fennel with peas, mint, parmesan and lemon
105 mixed mushrooms with farro, feta and almonds
109 winter tabbouleh with quinoa, sumac cauliflower, pomegranate and feta
141 pumpkin with chickpeas, toasted coconut and lemon tahini
153 zucchini noodles with asparagus, feta and mint

LEMONGRASS
65 hot and sour mung bean vermicelli with mushrooms, chinese cabbage and tofu
71 laksa hokkien noodles with green beans, chinese broccoli and tofu

LENTILS
43 pickled beetroot with puy lentils, baby spinach and cheddar
57 spiced sweet potato, puy lentils and rocket with honey walnuts
61 baked sweet potato with rocket, feta and black olive–walnut relish
75 spiced persian red lentils with roasted cauliflower and yoghurt
79 smoky baba ghanoush with roasted cauliflower, lentils and pomegranate
81 balsamic brussels sprouts and puy lentils with parmesan and mint
117 balsamic-roasted pears with lentils, gorgonzola and sage
119 puy lentils with balsamic-soaked figs, watercress and walnuts

LIMES
95 vietnamese cabbage salad with tofu, rice vermicelli and peanuts
97 thai kohlrabi and cabbage slaw with apple and crushed peanuts
147 barbecued corn and roasted pumpkin with black beans and jalapeño sour cream
165 hot and sour mung bean vermicelli with mushrooms, chinese cabbage and tofu
169 laksa hokkien noodles with green beans, chinese broccoli and tofu

LOTUS ROOT
83 chargrilled brussels sprouts with lotus root and sweet marinated tofu

MAPLE SYRUP
49 za'atar–roasted carrots with kale, freekeh and blood orange and maple dressing
83 chargrilled brussels sprouts with lotus root and sweet marinated tofu

MAYONNAISE
41 roasted beetroot with caramelised turnips, edamame and wasabi mayonnaise

MINT
65 chargrilled broccoli with chickpeas, almonds, lemon and chilli
81 balsamic brussels sprouts and puy lentils with parmesan and mint
93 cabbage and fennel with peas, mint, parmesan and lemon
109 winter tabbouleh with quinoa, sumac cauliflower, pomegranate and feta
121 peas and mint with quinoa, feta and almonds
153 zucchini noodles with asparagus, feta and mint
155 cucumber and tomatoes with haloumi and tzatziki

MISO
135 miso eggplant with soba noodles and walnuts

MUNG BEANS
53 honey–roasted carrots with mung beans and labneh

MUNG BEAN VERMICELLI
101 black fungus and five-spice tofu with mung bean vermicelli
161 seaweed with sesame, tofu and mung bean vermicelli
165 hot and sour mung bean vermicelli with mushrooms, chinese cabbage and tofu

MUSHROOMS

101 black fungus and five-spice tofu with mung bean vermicelli

103 pine mushrooms with eschalots, cherry tomatoes and sourdough croutons

105 mixed mushrooms with farro, feta and almonds

131 slow-roasted balsamic tomatoes with spelt pasta, porcini and ricotta

165 hot and sour mung bean vermicelli with mushrooms, chinese cabbage and tofu

NOODLES

115 spicy fried edamame with eggplant and soba noodles

135 miso eggplant with soba noodles and walnuts

163 soba noodles with shredded vegetables and ginger–shallot sauce

167 mie goreng with asian greens

169 laksa hokkien noodles with green beans, chinese broccoli and tofu

OLIVES

57 baked sweet potato with rocket, feta and black olive–walnut relish

127 baked tomatoes with capers, olives and croutons

155 cucumber and tomatoes with haloumi and tzatziki

ONIONS, BROWN

51 spiced roasted carrots with fennel and caramelised onion

75 spiced persian red lentils with roasted cauliflower and yoghurt

145 cinnamon pumpkin with chickpeas, tahini and candied pumpkin seeds

ONIONS, RED

49 za'atar–roasted carrots with kale, freekeh and blood orange–maple dressing

55 chargrilled fennel and asparagus with pearl couscous and coriander oil

87 ginger–peanut kale with tofu and quinoa

129 panzanella with heirloom tomatoes

ORANGES

49 za'atar–roasted with kale, freekeh and blood orange–maple dressing

PARMESAN

61 spiced sweet potato, puy lentils and rocket with honey walnuts

65 chargrilled broccoli with chickpeas, almonds, lemon and chilli

81 balsamic brussels sprouts and puy lentils with parmesan and mint

89 ribollita salad with kale, cavolo nero, fennel, tomatoes, cannellini beans and ciabatta

91 cavolo nero and borlotti beans with tomatoes, croutons and basil cream

93 cabbage and fennel with peas, mint, parmesan and lemon

103 pine mushrooms with eschalots, cherry tomatoes and sourdough croutons

127 baked tomatoes with capers, olives and croutons

129 panzanella with heirloom tomatoes

PARSLEY

59 moroccan sweet potato, chickpeas and couscous with chermoula

65 chargrilled broccoli with chickpeas, almonds, lemon and chilli

85 turnips, dutch carrots and cannellini beans with sunflower-seed pesto

73 roasted cauliflower with caper vinaigrette and lemon–parsley pangrattato

93 cabbage and fennel with peas, mint, parmesan and lemon

105 mixed mushrooms with farro, feta and almonds

109 winter tabbouleh with quinoa, sumac cauliflower, pomegranate and feta

153 zucchini noodles with asparagus, feta and mint

PASTA

67 broccoli and orecchiette with yoghurt and peas

123 sugar snap peas, jerusalem artichokes, cannellini beans and orecchiette with warrigal green pesto

PEAS

67 broccoli and orecchiette with yoghurt and peas

93 cabbage and fennel with peas, mint, parmesan and lemon

121 peas and mint with quinoa, feta and almonds

PEANUTS

87 ginger–peanut kale with tofu and quinoa

95 vietnamese cabbage salad with tofu, rice vermicelli and peanuts

97 thai kohlrabi and cabbage slaw with apple and crushed peanuts

159 nasi goreng with asian greens

173 gado gado with sate sauce

PEARS

117 balsamic–roasted pears with lentils, gorgonzola and sage

PEARL BARLEY

111 pearl barley with pistachios, rocket and basil oil

151 chargrilled zucchini and pearl barley with whipped feta and dill

PESTO

85 turnips, dutch carrots and cannellini beans with sunflower-seed pesto

123 sugar snap peas, jerusalem artichokes, cannellini beans and orecchiette with warrigal green pesto

PISTACHIO NUTS

111 pearl barley with pistachios, rocket and basil oil

149 fried zucchini with green couscous

POMEGRANATE

79 smoky baba ghanoush with roasted cauliflower, lentils and pomegranate

109 winter tabbouleh with quinoa, sumac cauliflower, pomegranate and feta

POPPY SEEDS

143 pumpkin with burnt butter, poppy seeds and crispy sage

POTATOES

47 roasted beetroot, shaved fennel and broad beans with skordalia

173 gado gado with sate sauce

PRESERVED LEMONS

59   moroccan sweet potato, chickpeas and couscous with chermoula

PUMPKIN

77   chargrilled cauliflower with fried butter beans and pumpkin hummus

141   pumpkin with chickpeas, toasted coconut and lemon tahini

143   pumpkin with burnt butter, poppy seeds and crispy sage

145   cinnamon pumpkin with chickpeas, tahini and candied pumpkin seeds

147   barbecued corn and roasted pumpkin with black beans and jalapeño sour cream

PUMPKIN SEEDS (PEPITAS)

53   honey–roasted carrots with mung beans and labneh

77   chargrilled cauliflower with fried butter beans and pumpkin hummus

123   sugar snap peas, jerusalem artichokes, cannellini beans and orecchiette with warrigal green pesto

145   cinnamon pumpkin with chickpeas, tahini and candied pumpkin seeds

147   barbecued corn and roasted pumpkin with black beans and jalapeño sour cream

QUINOA

69   sweet sesame broccoli and edamame with quinoa

87   ginger–peanut kale with tofu and quinoa

109   winter tabbouleh with quinoa, sumac cauliflower, pomegranate and feta

121   peas and mint with quinoa, feta and almonds

RICE

133   black bean eggplant with snake beans and brown rice

159   nasi goreng with asian greens

RICE VERMICELLI

95   vietnamese cabbage salad with tofu, rice vermicelli and peanuts

RICOTTA

131   slow-roasted balsamic tomatoes with spelt pasta, porcini and ricotta

ROCKET

57   baked sweet potato with rocket, feta and black olive–walnut relish

61   spiced sweet potato, puy lentils and rocket with honey walnuts

111   pearl barley with pistachios, rocket and basil oil

117   balsamic–roasted pears with lentils, gorgonzola and sage

149   fried zucchini with green couscous

SAGE

117   balsamic–roasted pears with lentils, gorgonzola and sage

143   pumpkin with burnt butter, poppy seeds and crispy sage

SEAWEED

161   seaweed with sesame, tofu and mung bean vermicelli

SESAME

41   roasted beetroot with caramelised turnips, edamame and wasabi mayonnaise

69   sweet sesame broccoli and edamame with quinoa

101   black fungus and five-spice tofu with mung bean vermicelli

161   seaweed with sesame, tofu and mung bean vermicelli

SHALLOTS

163   soba noodles with shredded vegetables and ginger–shallot sauce

SNOW PEAS

121   peas and mint with quinoa, feta and almonds

SOURDOUGH

103   pine mushrooms with eschalots, cherry tomatoes and sourdough croutons

127   baked tomatoes with capers, olives and croutons

SOUR CREAM

91   cavolo nero and borlotti beans with tomatoes, croutons and basil cream

147   barbecued corn and roasted pumpkin with black beans and jalapeño sour cream

SNAKE BEANS

133   black bean eggplant with snake beans and brown rice

141   pumpkin with chickpeas, toasted coconut and lemon tahini

SOBA NOODLES

115   spicy fried edamame with eggplant and soba noodles

163   soba noodles with shredded vegetables and ginger–shallot sauce

SPINACH

43   pickled beetroot with puy lentils, baby spinach and cheddar

45   beetroot and dill with crème fraiche and walnuts

65   chargrilled broccoli with chickpeas, almonds, lemon and chilli

73   roasted cauliflower with caper vinaigrette and lemon–parsley pangrattato

75   spiced persian red lentils with roasted cauliflower and yoghurt

103   pine mushrooms with eschalots, cherry tomatoes and sourdough croutons

SPRING ONIONS

45   beetroot and dill with crème fraiche and walnuts

149   fried zucchini with green couscous

153   zucchini noodles with asparagus, feta and mint

SUGAR SNAP PEAS

121   peas and mint with quinoa, feta and almonds

123   sugar snap peas, jerusalem artichokes, cannellini beans and orecchiette with warrigal green pesto

SUMAC

109   winter tabbouleh with quinoa, sumac cauliflower, pomegranate and feta

SUNFLOWER SEEDS

55 chargrilled fennel and asparagus with pearl couscous and coriander oil
85 turnips, dutch carrots and cannellini beans with sunflower-seed pesto

SWEET POTATOES

57 baked sweet potato with rocket, feta and black olive–walnut relish
59 moroccan sweet potato, chickpeas and couscous with chermoula
61 spiced sweet potato, puy lentils and rocket with honey walnuts

TABBOULEH

109 winter tabbouleh with quinoa, sumac cauliflower, pomegranate and feta

TAHINI

69 sweet sesame broccoli and edamame with quinoa
87 ginger–peanut kale with tofu and quinoa
141 pumpkin with chickpeas, toasted coconut and lemon tahini
145 cinnamon pumpkin with chickpeas, tahini and candied pumpkin seeds

TOFU

83 chargrilled brussels sprouts with lotus root and sweet marinated tofu
87 ginger–peanut kale with tofu and quinoa
95 vietnamese cabbage salad with tofu, rice vermicelli and peanuts
101 black fungus and five-spice tofu with mung bean vermicelli
161 seaweed with sesame, tofu and mung bean vermicelli
165 hot and sour mung bean vermicelli with mushrooms, chinese cabbage, and tofu
169 laksa hokkien noodles with green beans, chinese broccoli and tofu
171 spiced coconut with blanched vegetables
173 gado gado with sate sauce

TOMATOES

73 roasted cauliflower with caper vinaigrette and lemon–parsley pangrattato
89 ribollita salad with kale, cavolo nero, fennel, tomatoes, cannellini beans and ciabatta
91 cavolo nero and borlotti beans with tomatoes, croutons and basil cream
103 pine mushrooms with eschalots, cherry tomatoes and sourdough croutons
109 winter tabbouleh with quinoa, sumac cauliflower, pomegranate and feta
127 baked tomatoes with capers, olives and croutons
129 panzanella with heirloom tomatoes
131 slow-roasted balsamic tomatoes with spelt pasta, porcini and ricotta
137 roasted eggplant with sofrito, chickpeas and almonds
155 cucumber and tomatoes with haloumi and tzatziki

TURNIPS

41 roasted beetroot with caramelised turnips, edamame and wasabi mayonnaise
85 turnips, dutch carrots and cannellini beans with sunflower-seed pesto

TZATZIKI

155 cucumber and tomatoes with haloumi and tzatziki

VERMICELLI

95 vietnamese cabbage salad with tofu, rice vermicelli and peanuts
101 black fungus and five-spice tofu with mung bean vermicelli

VINAIGRETTE

73 roasted cauliflower with caper vinaigrette and lemon–parsley pangrattato

WALNUTS

45 beetroot and dill with crème fraiche and walnuts
57 spiced sweet potato, puy lentils and rocket with honey walnuts
61 baked sweet potato with rocket, feta and black olive–walnut relish
73 roasted cauliflower with caper vinaigrette and lemon–parsley pangrattato
119 puy lentils with balsamic-soaked figs, watercress and walnuts
135 miso eggplant with soba noodles and walnuts

WARRIGAL GREENS

123 sugar snap peas, jerusalem artichokes, cannellini beans and orecchiette with warrigal green pesto

WASABI

41 roasted beetroot with caramelised turnips, edamame and wasabi mayonnaise

WATERCRESS

119 puy lentils with balsamic-soaked figs, watercress and walnuts

WOMBOK (CHINESE CABBAGE)

101 black fungus and five-spice tofu with mung bean vermicelli
165 hot and sour mung bean vermicelli with mushrooms, chinese cabbage and tofu
167 mie goreng with asian greens
171 spiced coconut with blanched vegetables
173 gado gado with sate sauce

YOGHURT

53 honey–roasted carrots with mung beans and labneh
67 broccoli and orecchiette with yoghurt and peas
75 spiced persian red lentils with roasted cauliflower and yoghurt
155 cucumber and tomatoes with haloumi and tzatziki

ZA'ATAR

49 za'atar–roasted with kale, freekeh and blood orange–maple dressing

ZUCCHINI

149 fried zucchini with green couscous
151 chargrilled zucchini and pearl barley with whipped feta and dill
153 zucchini noodles with asparagus, feta and mint

CONTRIBUTORS

LUISA BRIMBLE
cover & food photography

A photographer whose distinctive images can be seen internationally. She is also Founder and Creative Director of *Alphabet Journal*.
www.luisabrimble.com

MARTHA ZAKARYA
art direction & publication design

Photographer, designer and art director, working across a variety of disciplines in the areas of fashion, music, art and lifestyle.
www.marthazakarya.com

ERIKA RAXWORTHY
cover & food styling

Graphic designer and food and interiors stylist. Erika is a home baker, compulsive crafter and has a popular food blog.
www.erikarax.com

MONICA PEN
chapter title page illustration

Freelance designer with a passion for vectors and fine detail. Her lively inspirations and illustrations are featured on her blog.
www.monicapen.com

AMANDA LEE DENNING
map illustration

Amanda Lee is a freelance graphic designer and illustrator. She also runs a boutique print and stationery design studio.
www.amanda-lee.com

A PLUM BOOK

Published in 2014 by
Pan Macmillan Australia Pty Limited
Level 25, 1 Market Street,
Sydney, NSW 2000, Australia

Level 1, 15–19 Claremont Street
South Yarra, Victoria 3141, Australia

First published in 2013 by
Arthur Street Kitchen

Text © 2013 Hetty McKinnon
Photography © 2013 Luisa Brimble

Cataloguing-in-Publication data is available from the National Library of Australia.

ISBN 9781743530405

order@arthurstreetkitchen.com
www.arthurstreetkitchen.com

Printed by 1010 Printing International Limited

_____

Text by Hetty McKinnon
Photography by Luisa Brimble
Art Direction & Publication Design by Martha Zakarya
Food & Props Styling by Erika Raxworthy
Chapter Title Page Illustration by Monica Pen
Map Illustration by Amanda Lee Denning

_____